FOREWORD & GENERAL INTRODUCTION

Dear Reader,

Welcome to **DOs** and **DON'Ts** in Japan. We hope you enjoy this very easy to read book. It is also our hope that if you are interested in Japan or you are coming here, our book will encourage you to study a little about Japan and perhaps act as a window to this incomparable country.

This book is not intended to be the "be-all" and "end-all" or even the final word on the **DOs** and **DON'Ts**; we daresay that others may take issue with some things. We ask that you, as the reader, do realize that many of its **DOs** and **DON'Ts** are based on life experiences as well as a certain amount of study and research by the author. Please do read it with this aim in mind and **DON'T** be too critical of what is written therein. We do hope that your window to Japan will be opened if even only part way.

Finally, all knowledge is dependent on other knowledge. I thank Kentaro Ohkawa and Masaki Morisawa, colleagues and friends, who gave comments and suggestions; and David Thane, translator and advisor.

In our introduction to Japan we will acquaint you with some of the more important developments that lead to Japan in the 21st Century. It is agreed by historians that probably the greatest era

dos & don'ts
in Japan

By
Richard L. Carpenter

Illustrations by

Paul Davis

ISBN 978-974-9823-44-6

Copyright 2008 © iGroup Press Co., Ltd.

Published in Thailand by
iGroup Press Co., Ltd.
100 Lang Sanamgolf Krungthep Kreetha Road
Huamark, Bangkapi, Bangkok 10240
Thailand
Tel: +66 2 3223678
Fax: +66 2 7211639
E-mail: info@igrouppress.com

Distributed by
Booknet Co., Ltd.
1173, 1175, 1177, 1179 Srinakharin Road
Suan Luang, Bangkok 10250
Thailand
Tel: +66 2 3223678
Fax: +66 2 7211639
E-mail: booknet@book.co.th

Printed and bound in Thailand by
Amarin Printing & Publishing Public Co., Ltd.

All rights reserved. No part of this publication may be reproduced, stored in a retrieval system, or transmitted in any form or by any means, electronic, mechanical, photocopying, recording or otherwise, without the prior permission of the publisher.

Thank you for buying this book. We welcome your comments.
Please send them to: Email: comments@book.co.th

dos & don'ts in JAPAN

CONTENTS

page	
1	Foreword & General Introduction
41	Shopping
53	Inns and Baths
61	Entertainment
71	Eating and Drinking
89	Characteristics and Traits
113	Festivals and Holidays
129	Religion
141	Doing Business
151	Climate
155	Useful Info
159	Words & Phrases

dos & don'ts **in JAPAN**

was the Meiji Period or also called the Meiji Restoration.

But first a word about the periods of history and how they are named. When an Emperor assumes the throne, he chooses a name for his reign that will typify the age or the feeling that he wishes to convey throughout his reign. So going from the present to the past we have:

- Heisei Period, "Peace Everywhere" - January 8, 1989 - present
- Showa Period, "Enlightened Peace" - December 25, 1926 - January 7, 1989
- Taisho Period, "Great Righteousness" - July 30, 1912 - December 25, 1926
- Meiji Period or Meiji Restoration, "Enlightened Rule" - September 8, 1868 - July 30, 1912
- Tokugawa Period - 1603 - 1867

and others prior to the Tokugawa Period

Japan is officially known as "Nippon" or "Nihon." The English naming came to the west from early trade routes. The Cantonese word for Japan is *"Jatbun"* and in the Malay language, *"Jatbun"* became *"Japang."* Then this word was brought to Europe in the 16th century by the first Portuguese traders out of Malacca. In 1577 the first recorded name in English was written as *"Giapan."*

The **Tokugawa Period** was named after Ieyasu Tokugawa, a general of great ability who was able to unite the country through his military prowess. The entire Tokugawa Period lasted 250 years and was marked by internal peace, political stability and economic growth. But any Japanese who had unintentional contact with foreigners would be subject to prosecution. Such was the country in that everything was tightly controlled.

Then the "Black Ships" came.........

On July 8, 1853, Commodore Matthew C. Perry steamed into Uraga Harbour just south of Tokyo. On his person, he carried a letter from President Fillmore demanding that Japan open up its country as a stopover for U.S.A. ships. Not only did the Japanese not have the armaments - Perry's ships were bristling with canon aimed at the shore - they did not have the expertise in dealing with a foreigner. They caved in to Perry's demands and thus was Japan changed forever. Now enter the Meiji Period.

The **Meiji Period**, beginning on September 8, 1868 and ending on July 30, 1912 - a period of 45 years - ushered Japan into the 20th century. It was during this era that Japan began its modernization and rose to the status of a world power.

It was also at this time, that the economic power of the great *"zaibatsu"* such as Mitsui and Mitsubishi and others reached new heights. With the *zaibatsu* working hand in hand with the government, Japan gradually took control of much of Asia's market for manufactured goods, beginning with textiles.

During this period, Japan engaged in the Sino-Japanese War (1894-1895) defeating both China and Korea. Then followed the Russo-Japanese War (1904-1905). Both helped to sow the seeds of colonialism with the occupation of the Korean peninsula and parts of China (Manchuria) prior to and during World War II. As a result of the Meiji transition or restoration, Japan emerged as the first Asian industrialized country. After the death of the Emperor in 1912, the Taisho Emperor acceded to the throne, thus beginning the Taisho Period.

While Europe and the United States were preoccupied with World War I, Japan extended its hegemony during the **Taisho Period** by declaring war on Germany and quickly occupying the German-held territories in China. Even though it did not directly engage in fighting Germany, by siding with the Allies, Japan emerged as the dominant power in Asia at the end of World War I. The Taisho Emperor died in 1926 ushering in the Showa Period, the longest period of all Emperors to date.

The **Showa Period** was ruled by Emperor Hirohito and as history books will show, this was a period of turmoil and unrest in the world because of World War II. To this day, Japan's hegemony, colonialism and atrocities committed in Asia are still rooted in people's memories.

The American occupation, preceded by the devastation of two atomic bombs, was led by General Douglas MacArthur and lasted until 1952. The most important event of this period was the adoption of a new constitution and its supporting legislation. Upon the signing of the Treaty of San Francisco in September 1951, Japan regained its independent sovereignty.

The 1950s saw the re-emergence of the "reformed" *zaibatsu* which once again became the juggernauts and engines of economic growth. The international companies that we know today, such as Sony, Toyota, Nissan, Honda, Mitsui, Mitsubishi, Sumitomo, NEC and many, many others were all revived during this period and have grown to become the powerhouses that they are now.

The period following Japan's economic "bubble," from about 1994 to the present, is known as the "Lost Decade" or "Lost Generation." GDP stagnated, real estate declined in value and all those loans made earlier were called in. It was "musical chairs" when it came to the Prime Minister's chair as Japan went through a continued procession of failed leaders.

At present, columnists and sociologists bemoan the fact that Japan has "lost its soul" and that the younger generation is only interested in Nintendos and immediate gratification causing all sorts of social problems. The "OLs" (office ladies) are the *nouveau riche* because they live at home with their parents saving their money to buy luxury clothes and accessories. They have been given the rather unflattering name of "parasites." And they're not breeding either. Society is aging at a fast pace putting in jeopardy the pensions all are looking forward to.

However in this author's eyes, Japan is still a good place to live and visit. Although expensive - Tokyo is voted the most expensive city (Osaka is second) just about every year - one can live modestly and well. It is relatively crime free and clean although one can find "dirt" in any corner if one looks. Immigration policies are still rather inward looking and Japan's bureaucracy still does not recognize the fact that outside (meaning immigrants) help may be necessary as society ages.

Welcome to Japan

Narita International Airport-The Gateway to Japan

As you approach Narita you do start to wonder, "Where's Tokyo? I don't see any tall buildings; Am I really landing in Japan?" Welcome to Narita International Airport, built from the expropriated land - and forcefully at times - of the farmers who lived in the area. **DO** understand that under your feet once grew rice, radishes and cabbages! Narita was a lesson in how not to do things in Japan. Only one of its runways can handle 747s while the other can handle only medium size jets. It's being extended - has been for about 20 years or so.

DO realize that Narita is approximately 60 kilometres from

Tokyo so **DO** steel yourself for *one more ride after arrival.*

Your first stop after deplaning will be Immigration. Next is Customs. Customs may or may not check your luggage. It is said they do a certain amount of profiling that determines whether your bags are checked or not. Choose the red or green channel not forgetting that allowances are generous. Duty free items include: three bottles of alcohol, 400 cigarettes, 2 oz. of perfume and up to ¥200,000 for other gifts. **DO** show your passport to the customs official.

DO realize that strictly prohibited items are illegal drugs and firearms. Japan is not kind to those who may try to smuggle in or use illegal drugs so **DON'T**! Beatle Paul McCartney was incarcerated for a week when illegal 'herbs' were found in his luggage.

After clearing Customs, exit through the doors immediately in front of customs. In the arrival area, you will find currency exchange and information on how to get to Tokyo.

Getting to Tokyo from Narita:

This may seem like a daunting task but despite the distance, it is relatively easy. The following are available:

Limousine Buses:

This is probably your best bet and kindest on your pocket. If your hotel is on one of the bus routes, purchase your ticket for that route. There is a map above the counter but **DO** ask the ticket agent. Or you can purchase a ticket to Tokyo City Air Terminal (TCAT) and at TCAT, take a taxi to your hotel. As sometimes there are traffic jams, the buses may be delayed so **DO** go to the restroom before getting on the bus!

Trains:

There are the (1) Keisei line, (2) Keisei Skyliner (super express), (3) Japan Railway (JR) Narita line and the (4) Narita Express (NEX). All lines are connected to the airport terminals *except* JR Narita line. The Keisei line connects to the Tokyo subway system and major transfer points (JR). The "Skyliner" goes directly either to Nippori or Ueno and then you must transfer at those stations to JR. JR Narita line connects to all major JR stations but you will need to take a taxi to Narita city to access this train line.

Taxis:

So is daddy taking care of all expenses as a graduation present or do you have a no holds-barred expense account? Then **DO** take a taxi, which is probably the easiest but the most *expensive* way into Tokyo. For the impecunious, which is most of us, the cost of a taxi ride, anywhere from ¥14,000 to ¥20,000 plus toll road charges and if late at night, late night charges, will easily add up to a couple of nights stay at a business hotel plus a few meals.

Narita has no domestic flights and so passengers will have to go to Haneda Airport which is within Tokyo city limits.

So to sum up, if you have limited budget, lots of baggage to carry, feel tired and don't feel like hassling with train transfers, **DO** take the limousine bus.

DON'T worry about being solicited for taxi rides or anything else but **DO** keep an eye on your luggage.

And a short note on departure:
DO note which terminal your flight leaves from as this will determine where you get off the bus or the train should you elect one of those means of transportation.

Staying in Japan

DO ensure you have the correct visa.

If you are going to be employed, **DO** apply for the proper visa and **DO** have your passport stamped with that visa prior to your departure from your native country. **DO** understand that Immigration frowns upon working with only a tourist visa as it is illegal and if discovered, you will be deported. So **DON'T** attempt this. Immigration checks have become stricter. But huge numbers of illegal workers still think it worth their while to play cat and mouse with the authorities.

For those residing in Japan, **DO** remember that you will have 90 days from entry date to apply for an Alien Registration

Certificate (called "ARC" or "Gaijin card" by locals) at your city or ward office. **DO** carry this card with you at all times, except possibly when bathing.

Some other airports - a quick bird's eye view from Kyushu to Hokkaido:

Fukuoka Airport

This is both a domestic and international airport and is considered a hub to East Asia. Very convenient - about 15 minutes to downtown.

Kansai International Airport

Coming into Kansai is almost like coming into the old Kai-Tak airport in Hong Kong (without the mountains and gut wrenching turn). It is completely surrounded by water as it was built on a man-made island in Osaka Bay and is connected by a causeway bridge. Contrary to rumours, it has not sunk into the bay quite yet although it is reported that the main supports *are* sinking ever so gradually. It is about 50 kilometres to the city of Osaka. The major disadvantage of Kansai International is that it has no domestic connections and so passengers must travel to Osaka Itami Airport for domestic flights, another hassle... (sigh)...

Chubu Centrair International Airport

This airport opened in February 2005, is also built on a man-made island in Ise Bay. It was actually constructed under budget and with strict adherence to preserving the surrounding environment. It is also said that it has taken business away from Kansai International Airport, something that Kansai is not too happy about!

Sapporo New Chitose Airport

Both a domestic and international airport, the airport is about 35 minutes to downtown.

Tokyo
Getting Around

Simply put, Japan is a commuter society. All major cities have excellent ground transportation that is clean, on time and relatively comfortable (except during rush hour). We will address Tokyo only but **DO** check out the systems in other major cities. Maps in English are printed so **DO** take the trouble to get one.

Subways

There are two major (and only) subway systems, The Metro and the Municipal system. **DO** note that lines are both colour coded as well as letter/number coded. Check out the map board in the stations above the ticket machines. Normally tickets are for one system or the other but if your destination is on the other system, **DO** press the "Transfer" button on the ticket machines and then press the correct fare button.

> Can't understand the map boards? Nowadays most stations have maps printed in English and these are usually (keyword) in a rack around the ticket machines. But if you don't see any maps, **DO** ask the attendant for one. And if you are really lost, feel free to ask the station attendant or another passenger. Most people are quite willing to help even if in rudimentary English.

When transferring, **DO** insert your ticket into the exit wicket and **DON'T** forget to take it with you when the machine regurgitates it on the other end, about three steps away. When arriving at your destination, once again insert the ticket into the machine as you exit and proceed on your way.

What to do if you don't know the correct fare? Easy! **DO** buy a minimum fare ticket and pay the difference at your destination at the "Fare Adjustment" machine.

And where is this Fare Adjustment Machine? It is usually found in the area near the exit wickets and it says right on top, **"Fair Adjustment"** - can't miss it!

What if you don't want to fool around with all this ticket business? Then **DO** purchase a "Passnet" pre-paid card. Just insert the card into the machine at your entry point and upon exiting, the machine will deduct the correct fare from the card. Easy! Cards can be bought in various amounts so **DO** inquire at the station or buy one from the ticket machine.

Ever wonder what happens to all of those used tickets? When you think about it, that's a lot of tickets! Well they are recycled and converted into toilet paper!

Above ground (JR and private lines)

All that we said about tickets and transfers etc. for the subways can be said for the JR and the private lines. JR has a pre-paid card as well so if you are using JR. **DO** purchase one for your daily use.

In Tokyo, the line that connects to all other major transfer points, long distant trains, the Shinkansen and points all around the city is the Yamanote Line or loop line. It is coloured green and can't be missed - the most convenient train in the city! Trains run about every 2-3 minutes during rush hour and about 5-6 minutes during other hours, so if you miss one, **DO** rest assured that another will be along shortly. In fact this is true of most trains in major cities.

If you will be living in Japan, **DO** purchase a "pass" either for 1, 3, or 6 months. The longer you take it, the more cost effective it is and the pass holder is allowed unlimited use of the pass on the route taken. If you go "outside," that is, your destination is a different one outside your route, then **DO** pay the extra fare at the fare adjustment machine. Just insert your pass into this machine and the calculation will be done automatically. Very easy! But **DO**

carefully safeguard your pass. If you lose it and it doesn't turn up somewhere then you will be crying in your *miso* soup when you have to purchase another one.

Private Railways are those owned and run by private corporations. These corporations also own the extensive property and buildings and holdings along the rail lines. They also own hotel chains, baseball teams, amusement parks and lots of other public facilities. So if you wish to ride a roller coaster or perhaps see "Kamen Rider" (popular with young kids) or maybe even "Godzilla" (rubber suited one - neither the real one nor Mr. Matsui of the Yankees) then **DO** check out the programs of the amusement parks.

Feel like trying to dodge a few fares? **DON'T**! And why not? All those tickets and passes are embedded with an electronic signal which the exit machine reads when you exit. If you still owe fare, you will be "binged-bonged" and the station attendant who is about two meters away is watching. So what to do? Surprise, surprise! Use the fare adjustment machine for automatic calculation of the remaining fare. There's even an "English" button you can press if you don't know what to do.

And while we are on the subject of trains, let us speak of the problem of groping. In the west it is assumed that if this problem were to occur, then the gropee would be able to take countermeasures or there will be those around her to help should this happen. However in Japan, psychologists say that gropers understand the crowd mentality and use it to their advantage. Women feel helpless when they are being touched in public and it is common that passengers around the woman, if they were to know what was going on, would ignore it. In a recent survey taken in Tokyo, of 630 Tokyo women who had been surveyed, 64 % had been groped but only 2% reported it to the police. There is also the prevailing reaction to *"naineiri"* or to "cry oneself to sleep," that is, the feeling that nothing can be done except suffer the humiliation. Seminars have been held by the police that teach passive tactics such as if and when touched, move away immediately or cough loudly to let the groper know that you know without drawing attention to the other passengers.

Another tactic is to remove his hand immediately and again to move away or to ask passengers around you to make some room. Since trains are overcrowded during the rush hours, it is really quite difficult at times to tell where the groping may be coming from so confrontation may not be the optimum choice.

So what to do?

DO keep in mind some of the suggestions noted in the above paragraph.

Some lines (including subways) have now designated the first and last cars as *"Women & Children only"* cars during rush hours. **DO** ride in these cars if available. It seems that the Japanese have finally

learned something from the Indians where "ladies only" cars have been standard for many years on commuter trains.

DO ride in a different car each day if you feel that you are being targeted. This is another suggested strategy. Gropers look for targets who stick to a routine.

If possible, **DO** stand or sit next to the end of the car with your back to the car if feasible or if touched, immediately move to the next car.

If you are the victim of groping, **DO** report it to the police. Even if you do not know who the groper is, it is best to report it in order to bring it to the attention of the authorities. If your Japanese language ability is not good enough to do so, **DO** bring a Japanese friend or acquaintance to help you.

If you *do know* the groper or the source, **DO** go to the station/platform attendant immediately. Understand though that Japanese language ability will be necessary in this case and time will be of the essence. If on the train and in between stations, one strategy is a nice downward thrust slowly and deliberately on his instep - aim carefully though - high heels are very effective.

Now back to getting around.....

Long distance trains and Shinkansen

Tickets for both kinds can be bought on the same day or in advance at the *midori madoguchi* or green window found in all stations. During the peak holiday seasons of New Year's and Obon (August) however, people line up at these windows to reserve seats for their trip back home. If you do not get a seat at these times, you will be guaranteed S.R.O. - and sometimes to 300% capacity of the train car. So **DO** try to book in advance if possible during these peak times.

Buses

For the adventurous **DO** try taking a bus. Most people ride the bus only for short distances. However you must know exactly where you want to go, which bus to take and where to get off. Sounds daunting? You bet...and there is no English help at all and it's doubtful that drivers speak that much English too. But, if you do use the bus, **DON'T** worry about not having exact change - the machines can give change, even for bills. Listen carefully to the announcements for the next bus stop and **DO** press the button on the wall to signal that you wish to get off. That's all.

Taxis

It is said that Tokyo taxis are the most expensive in the world. At the drop of the flag, the first ¥660 will take you 2 kilometres after which the meter will quickly climb. There is also a 20% increase between 11:00 p.m. and 5 a.m. Fares are regulated though; drivers are accommodating and will not try "to take you for a ride." So **DO** consider taking a taxi. Taxis can be hailed just about any place but take note that there are taxi ranks in front of stations and other public buildings and hotels etc.

And **DON'T** start getting fidgety when you see the meter turn over while sitting in traffic. It is programmed to do so. **DO** think about where you are going and what time of day you are going. It can be expensive unless you are on expense account or some Sugar Daddy is paying for the ride.

DON'T be surprised when the left rear door opens automatically to allow you to get in and **DO** let the driver close it as well.

If you take a toll road or expressway, **DO** pay the tolls in addition to the fare.

If you use a "call taxi," that is, a taxi that will come to pick you up, **DO** know that there will be a surcharge of ¥500.

> *If you have the business card of your destination, **DO** show it to the driver. However **DON'T** expect the driver to know all of the roads in Tokyo which is like a maze at times. If you are going to a different part of the city or one that may be outside the driver's expertise or knowledge, you may find yourself giving directions. **DO** see the back of this book for some helpful phrases.*

Bicycles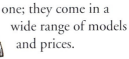

What is the most common form of private transportation in Japan? The bicycle of course! A rather high percentage of the population (we don't remember exactly) owns at least one bike. You **DON'T** need a license or need to take any kind of course. **DO** just go out to a department store or a bicycle shop and buy one; they come in a wide range of models and prices.

DO be careful when riding though. **DO** expect to run into (not literally of course...) the elderly, school children, housewives with one or two kids on their bikes, salaried men hurrying to the station, and cops on their white bikes

and just about everybody else, although we haven't seen any dogs pedalling bikes yet... People ride on the sidewalk (most common place) on the side of the roads where there are no sidewalks, with the traffic, against the traffic, going through red lights and stop signs and well...we hope you get the picture. **DO** be careful on narrow neighbourhood streets as you will be competing with cars, other bike riders and pedestrians. **DO** slow down at blind corners and **DON'T** assume that no-one else is coming from the cross-street. **DO** expect that bike riding can be hazardous to one's health if you're not careful. Other than the foregoing it's a great way to get to the supermarket or *sakaya* (liquor store) for your beer and back in time for your favourite TV programs!

And finally **"My Car."**

Japanese love their "my car." **DON'T** expect to see any junks or "beaters" on the roads. And **DON'T** expect any dirty or dented cars or rust buckets either! **DO** expect to see new or late model cars, clean, polished and possibly with an extra antenna or two and nowadays with a GPS system. **DON'T** be surprised if you see the driver watching TV while driving!

First, Japanese drive on the LEFT side of the road.

Second, owning a car in Japan is expensive. **DON'T** be shocked at the taxes, the cost of gas (2/3 of the price is also taxes), the cost of a simple oil change, the weight and road taxes and **DON'T** go into shock when you see your bill from the mandatory inspections. If you live in the city you may not need a car but if you do have one, **DO** be aware that you have to have proof of a *legal* (keyword here) parking space such as a garage attached to your home or a rented space etc. And **DON'T** choke on your disbelief when you learn how much it costs to rent a space in the city!

Third, **DO** check with the Japan Automobile Federation (JAF) on the **DOs** and **DON'Ts** of converting your overseas license into a Japanese license. And if you are required to take a driver's-ed course **DO** be patient and follow the course outline and **DON'T** expect to pass right away. There are regular courses for those not in a hurry, a speeded up course for those with less time to spare and a super-express course for those in a super rush...all for a fee of course. Driving schools abound in Tokyo so **DO** check or **DO** ask around for the best and most accommodating and perhaps cheapest school.

To sum up, **DO** realize that owning a hunk of steel on four wheels in Japan - and especially in the city - can be an expensive proposition.

Where to stay?

Tokyo is a huge cosmopolitan city and does not lack for hotels. Going first class? Then there is the Hilton, the Imperial and Hyatt to name just a few. There are many, many others and our apologies if they are not named here. If you have limited budget, check out the so-called "business hotels" that are everywhere and usually located in the vicinity of a station. The single rooms in these hotels are well, small - four steps and you're across the room. However they are clean, well lit, safe and have basic facilities for your stay. They're a place to "hang your hat" and get a good night's sleep and they are quite affordable for Tokyo. So **DO** do a search online or ask your travel agent about them. Doubles and twins are also available.

There are also *ryokans* or inns but they are much harder to find and are way off the beaten path and do not necessarily advertise their whereabouts. Due to the high cost of real estate in Tokyo, Japanese inns are a dying breed indeed. If you wish to experience one **DO** read further in this book!

If your budget is really limited, there are the "capsule hotels." These hotels are really for those who may be working late into the night and cannot get home, those who went out drinking and missed the last train home and those looking for a place to sleep at a very cheap price. They are literally capsules but do have all the amenities and some even have saunas. These are *not* recommended however after a long flight and besides finding one would be a problem.

And for the really budget conscious person, there is the Japan Youth Hostels, Inc. An overnight stay is around ¥3,500 per night but one must have a membership card. To find out the particulars in English, just go to Japan Youth Hostels, Inc. on the internet. Hostels are strictly segregated so married couples...sorry no sleeping together here.

Finally there are the "love hotels" found in the garish parts of the city and along toll ways and they are for...well we think you can guess what they are for! You can stay by the night - if you so wish - which is much cheaper than by the hour but **DO** be prepared for a certain amount of noise caused by unguarded moments, giggles, and the opening and closing of doors throughout the night. Don't ever say we didn't tell you so.

Things to do and places to see

Just take a look at a map of Tokyo and you'll be struck by the asymmetry of the city. Tokyo is not on a grid. It looks more like a maze. However, **DO** notice that all roads go more or less in a circle or oval. Why? Look again and **DO** notice that patch of green in the centre: the Emperor's palace grounds where he and his family presently live. And for those who are interested in such things, there is a rather high percentage of the crow population that also lives in these grounds so the Emperor is not alone.

Even subways **DON'T** pass under the royal compound. It is prohibited of course to enter the grounds except on two occasions, the Emperor's birthday (December 23rd) and New Year's (January 1st). It is possible to walk around the perimeter, a walk of approximately four kilometres. As one walks, one can get a feel for the city and its various cityscapes. And if during cherry blossom season, it is quite beautiful as walkways and parks are decked out in pretty shades of pink.

There is Hibiya Park across the street from the Imperial Hotel, the old hotel being famous because of its design by Frank Lloyd Wright. Sorry, it was demolished around 1968 but a few remnants were shipped to Meiji Mura (village) located near Nagoya as part of the permanent exhibit there. However **DO** go into the Old Imperial Bar which still retains some of the décor from the original hotel and have a drink while taking in the atmosphere.

And then there is the Ginza (**DO** see "shopping" in this book) - all we can say is **DO** go before sunset, walk around the famous Ginza intersection and watch as the area turns into a sea of brilliant and colourful neon lights, famous around the world. And **DON'T** forget your camera!

Would you like to get a feel for a shrine or temple? While Tokyo is dotted with shrines and temples - not to the extent as Kyoto is however - there is Asakusa Kannon Temple and Meji Jingu Shrine. The former is Buddhist and the latter, Shintoist. Asakusa Kannon Temple is one station on the Ginza or Toei subway lines (Asakusa Station) and Meiji on the Chiyoda subway line (Meiji Jingu Mae) or JR Yamanote line (Harajuku Station). At Asakusa you may see a mendicant Buddhist trainee standing to one side, bell in one hand and bowl in the other. As part of his training, he is begging for alms, so if moved, **DO** drop a coin or two in his bowl. Upon receipt, he will offer a prayer or two in your favour. **DO** take in the various images and statues of both locations. Walk up to the main entrance of the temple - you cannot go inside however - throw a coin into the box, clap your hands three times and say a short prayer for whatever or whomever you wish. Pictures are OK to take. If there are large incense burners outside, **DO** step up to the side and "gather" some of the smoke and "spread" it over itself. The smoke is for cleansing yourself prior to approaching the entrance of the temple.

Another shrine is the famed Yasukuni Shrine - the one that former Prime Minister Koizumi visits every year - that houses the ashes of soldiers from previous wars and is a subject of continued dispute between Japan, Korea and China.

Go to any station during rush hour and feel the waves of humanity as people rush hither and yon trying to get to work on time. Shinjuku Station alone has about 3.22 million people pass through it every day - just imagine the entire city of Chicago (pop. 2.92 million) emptying out in one day! Shinjuku is the busiest train station in the world. Do you want to physically feel the crush of rush hour? then **DO** take the Yamanote line during peak hours. **DO** read the groping section again!

Tokyo Station is huge and is the hub for the Shinkansen, commuter trains, long distance trains and suburban commuter trains. Are you a train buff? Then **DO** go to Tokyo Station, buy a platform ticket and bring your camera. You won't be dissatisfied.

When people think of Tokyo, they see only tall buildings, masses of people, activity to the likes of worker bees and noise and traffic and all those things associated with big cities but more massively and densely packed. Go into another part of the city and walk around - if you have a map all the better - you will find narrow streets, quiet lanes, houses tucked away in small cul-de-sacs, small gardens behind old wooden fences, laundry hung out to dry on balconies or verandas, patches of sunlight breaking through shady areas and... in other words, sometime visitors almost never get to see the other side of Tokyo and it does

exist and it is different and it does give one an entirely different perspective on the city. So if you have time to spare and like to explore, **DO** get off the beaten track. Take a train or a subway away from the centre of the city or ride the Yamanote line and get off at the smaller stations and walk around.

DO go to Odaiba that was built on reclaimed land out of Tokyo Bay and is now a popular spot for all seasons for shopping, walking along the beach, visiting Fuji TV Building or just plain hanging out. **DON'T** go swimming in Tokyo Bay - not recommended due to water quality.

Disneyland - ah yes, Disneyland accessible by train, bus and car and easy to get to - a world famous mouse is waiting.

Did you know that Tokyo has its own radio and TV tower modelled after the Eiffel Tower? Yes, it's Tokyo Tower, 333 meters and is the world's tallest self supporting iron tower. And here's something for the "I-bet-you-didn't-know-this-file." It weighs just a mere 4,000 tons coming in under the Eiffel Tower which weighs in at 7,000 tons. Anyway if you wish a bird's-eye view of the city - on a clear day of course - **DO** purchase a ticket and take the elevator up to the first landing. And on a very clear day, one can even see Mt. Fuji.

Takarazuka...what's that you say? Shouldn't this be in the entertainment section? Yes, but Takarazuka is something to see and it is an all women's revue, officially named Takarazuka Revue Company. Without going into detail, suffice it to say that young women enter the company and undergo rigorous and strict training to become part of the troupe. The revue company puts on many stage musicals based on historical episodes or more modern "Guys and Dolls" fare where the all the players, are of course, "she". If you want to sense the flavour of this particular institution, **DO** purchase a ticket but **DON'T** be surprised to see hundreds of women patiently waiting outside the theatre entrance in order to get a glimpse of their favourite star as she arrives.

A nice place to spend a couple of hours is Tokyo International Forum close to Yurakucho JR station. This Forum is the site for concerts, cultural events, exhibitions, trade fairs but the main reason it is well known is that it was designed by renowned architect Rafael Vinoly using glass and steel. The whole structure resembles one huge ship and it is a pleasure to sit inside and watch as the sun passes overhead. **DO** check it out.

What place handled 615,409 tons of fish and fish products valued at 498 billion yen in 2003? It is Tokyo's Tsukiji Fish Market. This is something different and a visit is recommended before 9:00 a.m. Unfortunately the real action, the auctioneering and the buying and selling and hustle and bustle that begins around 5:00 a.m., is closed to tourists. After visiting the market, go to one of the sushi restaurants and have sushi for breakfast!

And something different: **Food Theme Parks**

Ikebukuro Gyoza Stadium:

What are gyoza? They are a kind of fried Chinese dumpling with chopped pork and chives and perhaps some garlic inside. The Stadium is located near Ikebukuro Station. There is a small entrance fee and about 20 different gyoza shops inside, all reasonably priced.
Telephone: 03-5950-0765

Yokohama Curry Museum:

Located near Kannai Station (JR) in Yokohama, one can learn about the history of curry (a very popular dish in Japan) as well as sample various curries at the restaurants inside. Telephone: 045-250-0833

Shin-Yokohama Ramen Museum:

The interior of this museum is one of an old downtown area in Tokyo and one can eat various kinds of *ramen* (noodles) from around Japan. Telephone: 045-471-0503

And here are three more and different museums to see:

Toy Museum located in Tokyo. This museum has over 8,000 toys on display reflecting cultural tastes and times. Telephone: 03-3874-5133

Kite Museum located near the Ginza in Tokyo. According to the web site, this museum is literally covered from floor to ceiling with kites. Kites are a part of the culture in Japan, mainly being flown around New Year's time and they range from very tiny to huge ones with long attached cords. They are colourfully decorated and beautiful to see against a clear blue sky during the New Year's holidays.

And for something really weird, we have the...

Meguro Parasite Museum in Tokyo. Are you into tapeworms - apparently the longest tapeworm on record in Japan is in enshrined here - mosquitoes, cock roaches, mites, lice and weird photos? Then **DO** go to this museum. Telephone: 03-5489-9471.

Four quick one day trips outside of Tokyo:

Hakone National Park: Call the Odakyu Sightseeing Service (Tel: 3-5321-7887) and make reservations on the "Romance Car" for the Fuji Hakone Pass. Your trip will also include a cable car ride over the hills and valleys and up to Owakudani, known for its fumaroles and its very strong sulphur smell. **DO** buy a "black egg" there - an egg that has been boiled and turns black because of the mineral content.

Yokohama City: Accessible by any number of train routes, Yokohama has a long history as one of the main ports of Japan going back to the days of sailing ships. **DO** walk around Yamashita Park, Motomachi Street and stop in at the Yokohama Silk Museum. Go up to the "Bluff" and tour a restored Meiji era house and take a look at *Gaijin Bochi* (foreigners' cemetery) nearby.

Kamakura: Kamakura, once the seat of the government in the 13th century, is a lovely town about 1 hour by train south of Tokyo. It is located at the top of Sagami Bay and boasts nice beaches with the typical scene of a coastal town during the summer and a countrified atmosphere sprinkled with temples and shrines. **DO** visit Hachimangu and the Great Buddha, both main attractions of this town. If you're wanting a quieter atmosphere, go one train stop to Kita-Kamakura and stroll through this small and intimate town. Visit the temples and shrines that are all located within a short walking distance from each other. Kita-Kamakura is the site of Engakuji Temple, the setting for Yasunari Kawabata's novel, *"Thousand Cranes."*

Do you just want to get a general feel for the city without the hassle of getting around the city? Hato Bus offers all kinds of tours (English tours also available) so **DO** *check this out.*

Nikko National Park: Approximately a two hour train ride from Asakusa Station, Nikko offers landscapes, waterfalls, temples and shrines all within walking distance. The main drawing card is the mausoleum of Ieyasu Tokugawa, known as Toshogu Shrine. Other shrines and temples are all in the vicinity. Go in the autumn and enjoy the beautiful colours. Hike your way around the town and take in the various and sundry shops and return home in the evening knowing that you have visited a special place.

> *In order to avoid some of the hassle of buying tickets at each place you go to, you can buy a "one day pass" for the subways for one price. This allows unlimited use of the subway for one day and can be a quite efficient way to get around. However* **DO** *plan your itinerary before undertaking this.*

A Little Bit of Tokyo Living

An entire book could be written about this very topic and suffice it to say that there are a number of books on the market that go into great detail. We recommend that you **DO** read the sections on shopping, entertainment and the Japanese as these could also come under the heading of Tokyo living. However we will just try and hit some salient points.

Tokyo can be one huge jumble or maze for the foreigner just off the plane. Certainly if you have a support system of some kind, this will help to ease one into this mass of humanity called Tokyo.

As said earlier, if coming to work, **DO** ensure that you have the proper visa. Lots of foreigners come to Japan to teach English. Without getting into a lot of details, basic requirements are (1) a college degree, (2) a sponsor (could be your employer if so agreed) and (3) the proper visa. There are a number of forums one can access that give the pluses and minuses of teaching in Japan (see back of book). **DO** read these forums carefully and then formulate your own opinions about whether you wish to follow this particular employment path or not.

DO remember that you have to apply for your Alien Registration Card at the local city or ward office and **DON'T** forget that any changes of address or status, e.g., getting married, visa status and such also must be reported to these offices. The people who work in these offices are usually quite helpful - even more so than dour Immigration. Oh well. **DO** visit the website of the Ministry of Foreign Affairs of Japan, which details types of visas and requirements.

One of the first requirements will be a place to live. **DON'T** assume that landlords are happy to rent to foreigners. Regardless of how much Tokyo presents itself as an "international city" it is quite provincial in many ways and this goes for landlords. **DO** expect to experience some rejection - because you are of the wrong race - until you find a helpful realtor and willing landlord. Also read the classified ads in papers and mags for foreigners. And then there are the costs of *shikikin* (deposit) and *reikin* (thank you payment), usually to the tune of 2 to 3 months in advance.

When moving into a new place, it is customary to bring a little gift, sweets or the like, to those neighbours who live in the closest proximity to you. **DON'T** *overdo it; just some little inexpensive gift will do fine.*

There is no lack of stores for the staples of living. Most neighbourhoods will have some sort of "shopping street," so **DO** stroll through these and pick up what you need. There are regular supermarkets, some hypermarkets, lots of mom and pop stores, convenience stores and ¥100 stores. **DO** load up with plastic containers and napkins and kitchen things and ball pens - well you name it! ¥1,000 goes a long way in these stores.

While most people buy tofu (soy bean curd) at the supermarket nowadays, in some neighbourhoods the tofu man comes through blowing his off-tune horn (or so it seems). *"Tofuuu....tofuuu,* fresh *tofuuu"* you can almost hear the horn sing. This tofu is freshly made and can be bought right then and there. So **DO** have a bowl ready for the block of tofu.

Thirsty from all that walking about? You won't have to look far for a vending machine. Tokyo is filled with them - juice, tea, coffee in cans, soft drinks, cigarettes, beer, yes *beer*! from machines. There are even machines that sell eggs, rice, comics, books, soft porn, neckties and in some parts of the city, underwear and other unmentionables. And in some dark part of the city or for all we know right out on Main street, there is a vending machine that sells used panties...just for the aficionado. And in love hotels, they sell, ummm, condoms - safe sex you know! But drinks machines of all kinds are in the majority. It is estimated that about 5% of Tokyo's electric power is eaten up by vending machines. Just like the little ditty - they're everywhere! - they're everywhere!

Japanese love their pets. Pet shops abound and there are shops that sell exotic pets, such as iguanas and other such reptiles. Despite all these pets, people are pretty careful about cleaning up after their dogs and so **DON'T** worry too much about stepping in something that is squishy and smelly.

And we hope that you don't mind crows. There is a "no kill" policy (unlike Singapore) and crows have propagated into the thousands. The only way they can be removed is to call the ward office and they will come and remove the nests. Crows being rather wily birds know where all the goodies, that is vittles, are and on any early morning you can find packs of them in and around all the restaurant areas that are near the major stations. **DON'T** ever cross a crow during nesting time as it becomes very aggressive. They will remember you and if they see you out, will dive bomb you from behind - scary to say the least. There was the story of some old lady, who was dive bombed, and started to wear a motorcycle helmet whenever she went out. And crows have these huge beaks, like some people we know.

There is a system of police boxes through out the city. These are called *koban* and will be manned usually by one or two policemen. If moving into a new neighbourhood, a cop may come around and ask for some family information along with phone numbers, etc. This is strictly for use in cases of emergency (or so we are told) and for the police to get to know the neighbourhood and who is living in it. So **DON'T** balk at having to fill out this form. The police are generally helpful and the idea behind the koban is to instil a sense of security in the area.

No book about Japan would be complete without something in it about garbage. In large cities, garbage is separated into: (1) burnables, (2) recyclables and (3) unburnables. In addition **DO** take note:

For large items such as furniture and the like - and it is not unusual to see used furniture put out for garbage collection - there is a special pickup service that must be contacted. The phone number is noted on the posters at the collection site. If in doubt **DO** ask your neighbour or the city or ward office. **DON'T** look upon this furniture as a newly found treasure and cart it away however.

Computers are handled as special cases and are to be recycled back to the manufacturer. Once again **DO** call for information on disposal of such.

All garbage has to be placed in special white bags that can be purchased anyplace. Some neighbourhoods have "garbage patrols" (no joke) that check the garbage to ensure that it is sorted properly. Stories abound of either *obaachans* (grandmas) or *ojiichans* (old geezers) who do the patrolling and checking. If they see someone putting out improperly sorted garbage, they will "return to sender." So **DO** take special care to follow the rules. After all its purpose is to reduce the overall waste in Tokyo (a serious problem) and help the environment although the Japanese have a mania for packaging. **DO** watch out for those *obaachans* or *ojiichans* though - "no mercy" is their slogan!

Yokohama City has even stricter rules and a rather thick manual of the **DOs** and **DON'Ts** of garbage separation. This manual is also available in English we understand.

Earthquakes...well living in Tokyo, means experiencing

earthquakes or, temblors as they are called, from time to time. Now to add to your sense of safety, experts say that the Great Kanto Earthquake is well overdue so **DO** be aware of this. Simply said, earthquakes are scary whether one is in a one floor house or 30 stories up. If a serious quake occurs, here are some things to remember:

DON'T use the elevator if in an office building. If outside, **DO** watch for falling glass.

If at home, **DO** ensure the gas or heater is turned off. **DO** open a door or window for possible escape. **DON'T** use matches or a lighter for light; if there is a gas leak, then it's bye-bye. If trapped at home, **DO** get under (quickly though) some sturdy furniture like a kitchen table to avoid being hit from falling objects. **DO** at all times have a flashlight with extra batteries, a three day supply of bottled water, freeze dried noodles or canned goods and **DO** keep these things in an easy-to-reach place.

Expect to be stared at. Tokyo is not so bad nowadays in this respect but if you are in the country, it comes with the territory. After all we are in their country and we **DO** stand out in more ways than one so **DO** expect this but **DON'T** let it bother you too much, even if your mommy brought you up never to stare at another. It goes without saying of course that other Asians, or more correctly Koreans or Chinese, will not be stared at.

Noise! **DO** expect to be bombarded with noise - lots of it!
"The elevator door is now closing. Be careful not to catch your hand/finger in it." "Be sure to stand in the middle of the step on the escalator and hold your child by the hand."

Instructions for this and instructions for that again and again.

Vending machines that talk as they welcome you to their vending machine, telling you to insert your coins into the slot and then wait for the change and then tell you that the change is now coming out and then thank you for using the vending machine.

Station platforms are a cacophony of noise - bells, whistles, music, announcements not once or twice but sometimes thrice! "Such and such a train is now approaching. Be sure to stand behind the white (or yellow) line." And on rainy days, "be sure not to forget your umbrella." and as you exit, "be sure to watch your step as there is a space between the car and the platform."

Squeak, jingle, boom-boom, pound, announce, blah-blah-blah.........And on it goes.

And one is not immune on ski slopes according to some skiers we know. There are birds chirping and music playing as you schuss your way down the slope.

Many years ago a famous Zen temple in Kyoto - Ryoanji with its famous rock garden - had a loudspeaker that incessantly explained about the garden and its meaning on and on and on......until one day people began to complain and it was removed. It is almost a contradiction when you think about it - Zen with its quiet and contemplation and a loudspeaker blaring away in one of the supreme Zen spots.

During election time **DO** buy a pair of earplugs - politicians or ladies speaking in very high voices repeating the same message again and again, "Tanaka, Tanaka, Tanaka vote for Tanaka. We ask your support...Tanaka, Tanaka....." They cruise the back streets of Tokyo in their little vans (and *very loud* speakers) filled with additional ladies wearing white gloves waving at everybody they see, even dogs. The urge to strangle somebody is very strong at these times...

And while on the subject of noise, you will be literally be blown off the street if any right wingers come around in their black buses with HUGE speakers blaring WWII military songs and marching songs. These folks know no bounds when it comes to getting their message across. Yes, there is a law in Japan about the amount of allowable decibels but the police turn a blind eye for reasons best not explained in this book. **DO** ignore these folks if at all possible even though you won't be able to ignore their noise.

SHOPPING

Bargaining is not the rule in Tokyo although in the Kansai area, it is more accepted. So **DON'T** try to bargain at department stores as prices are fixed. For other stores however if you feel the clerk just might give a break on the price, **DO** ask for the store to pay the 5% consumption tax. The possible exception to this might be Akihabara (noted below). If buying a number of items, the sales clerks in Akihabara will do a certain amount of bargaining in order to secure the sale. Competition is very keen there. So **DO** try in these situations if you feel it worth it.

Credit cards are accepted at the major stores but **DO** be prepared to pay cash. Japanese still prefer paper to plastic.

DO bring your passport for those stores that offer duty free items (for tourists only). It will be necessary for the paperwork that accompanies these items for export out of Japan.

DON'T smoke in stores or other public places as it is now against the law.

Generally people do line up but **DON'T** get upset if they don't and **DO** expect a bit of jostling in crowded areas and streets. After all there are approximately 12 million souls in Tokyo.

There are so many places in Tokyo to shop and to satisfy all of your desires that it really is impossible to name them all. Tokyo is famous for its various department stores, some of which have hundreds of year's history behind them. There is Mitsukoshi, Matsuya, Takashimaya, Matsuzakaya, Tobu, Tokyu, Seibu, Odakyu, Daimaru to name just some of the main ones. And usually they are located near train or subway stations.

Ginza. The entire Ginza area has not only department stores but it is known for its brand name goods. A stroll down Ginza Street towards the famous Ginza intersection will reveal the following: Matsuya Department, art galleries, bridal shops, stationery shops, jewellery stores, beer halls, restaurants, coffee shops, Tiffany, Cartier, Mikimoto Pearls, Chanel, YSL, Luis Vuitton, Opaque clothing, Fendi, banks, Burberry, Tasaki pearls, and others. Go to the intersection and on one side will be Mitsu-koshi Department Store with their reclining lion out front - a favourite meeting spot - and on the other side is Waco Department Store famous for its window displays, changed throughout the year. So **DO** walk through Ginza and take in all of the high priced items and displays of opulence and rich and famous looking brand names and know that you are walking on some of the highest priced real estate in Japan, except possibly Takano's Fruit Parlour, a store that sells fruit and sits right next to Shinjuku Station. At Takano's you will experience 'sticker shock' if you see the prices on some of their melons. It is rumoured that if you buy one of the more expensive melons, the price includes a security guard to accompany you home.

And when you get a little hungry, look for the little Yoshinoya *Gyudon* (beef ball) shop nestled in there among all these high rollers and **DO** order the *gyudon* for a pedestrian ¥420. Or if you prefer something more western, the Golden Arches are down the cross street from the intersection. Go a little farther to Higashi Ginza towards the *Kabukiza* (Kabuki theatre) and on the corner you will see Montana Pachinko Parlour. It's been there for years - we don't know why it's named Montana, Montana being associated with blue skies and mountains and pachinko parlours being quite the opposite of that...noisy and smoky. So if adventurous **DO** go inside and try your luck at pachinko. It's a real trip.

Most department stores have English speakers to assist foreign shoppers so **DO** approach the information desk. It seems that there are a lot of women who work at the department stores so for the men **DON'T** feel uncomfortable if looking for some outerwear or inner wear! Just smile away as she measures your inseam up to your crotch for that suit you are ordering. The ladies are all there to help you in your selections. The department stores usually have brand name cosmetics - usually on the 1st floor - so go and sniff your way around these floors.

All of the department stores have a food floor usually located on the B1 level and they have 'time service' sales as well on a daily

basis. So if looking for some good quality food, **DO** wait for these 'time service' sales and get a good price on your food shopping. And there are samples - lots of them! - to be sampled and ladies offering this or that so **DON'T** be shy and **DO** try them. You could almost have a small meal with all the samples. There was one foreigner who bragged that she often ate lunch on all these samples and made the rounds, a different department store each day... sort of like a homeless person, we suppose.

There are bargains - called bargain sale - at department stores throughout the year and especially at year end. **DO** expect to be pushed, shoved, elbowed, shouted at, jostled and whatever other verb you can think of during these times. It's every man, woman and child for him/herself.

At New Year's time, stores offer a *fukubukuro* or 'lucky shopping bag.' For a fixed price customers buy a bag of goodies and take their chances on what's inside. Of course the stores **DON'T** put in anything that is cheap or tacky. So it's kind of fun to see what one gets when buying the lucky shopping bag. There is big demand for these so **DO** go early and get in line.

And if there is a department store supporting the winner of the Japan Baseball Series, **DO** get ready for a huge sale. *Everything* will be on sale to celebrate the winning team. When the Hanshin Tigers won the pennant, the Hanshin Group raked in hundreds of jillions of yen at their department stores in Osaka.

Mind you the Ginza is not the only place; all of the main stations have tons of shopping around them. **DO** be adventurous, take your time and enjoy window shopping.

Do you like underground? Well then the **Tokyo Station Arcade** is for you. Extending out - underground of course - from the Yaesu side of Tokyo Station (Daimaru Department Store side) - about half kilometre in each direction, you will find all kinds of shops. Prices are fixed but one can be assured of quality as most shoppers in this area are the office workers who pass through to Tokyo Station. There are not only shops but also restaurants and drinking places and one or two liquor stores and of course those golden arches again... One can spend at least a couple of hours in the arcade just browsing and passing the time.

Going to the very humble subject of books, the **Jimbocho/Kanda** area is known for book stores. The main street is Yasukuni Doori (street) since Yasukuni Shrine is located at the top of it. It is sad to say that due to the somewhat declining book trade, some stores have locked their shutters for good or have redone their stores over into something else, like a sporting goods store. However there are still plenty of stores left. You will find newly

released titles, lots of second hand books, antiquarian books, wood block prints and books in English and Japanese and occasionally in other languages as well. If you are looking for a specific antiquarian item, go to Antiquarian Book Association of Japan (ABAJ) on the web for a directory of authorized dealers.

There is a famous brush shop - for calligraphy brushes - at the top of the area that has been in business for many years and the owner is said to have an original Picasso somewhere in his shop, Picasso having visited to buy brushes at one time. But if looking for real bargains **DO** wait until the end of October when there will be an outdoor book bargain sale with stalls and wagon carts loaded to the gills with all kinds of books. **DON'T** worry about having to schlep the books home as there is *takkyubin* (parcel delivery service) available to pack and send your books for you. There are cultural events and book signings and all kinds of things to do as well.

DO walk along Yasukuni Doori a little farther and you come to lots of sporting goods equipment stores, from trekking to outdoor sports, to body building, to surfing, skating, skiing - lots of things to choose from at reasonable prices. And when approaching the intersection that has Sanseido Book Store on one side and a guitar store on the other, the street goes uphill at that point. Of course you can continue on straight if you wish up the hill to see the ten different musical instruments store - mainly guitars but there is violin store and a wind instrument store as well. Looking for a cheap guitar for ¥15,000 or a pricey Fender at umpteen thousands of yen? You will find it here. **DON'T** worry about communication problems. Most shopkeepers can speak rudimentary English.

Looking for retro? Shimokitazawa is the place, a little train stop not too far from Shinjuku located on either the Inokashira or Odakyu train lines. This is a haven for the young crowd. If retro is you, swoon as you wander the very narrow streets crammed with all that is associated with 'yesterday chic'. There are jazz places and little pubs and used record shops as well. Great place to watch people too!

Fashion, fashion, *young fashion*, jeans, tops, shoes, cute, cool, fun, faddish, crazy, chill out, Hello Kitty, British punk, rebellious - you'll find it all in **Harajuku**. Takeshita street right opposite the station is jammed with shops and the young, young, young. On Sundays going over to the main street, Omotesando Doori, it becomes crowded with street performers. You will see young girls dressed in Gothic style, with bleached hair, greyed hair down to their shoulders, false eyelashes, pink wigs, piercings in visible parts of the body, boys in jeans hanging from their hips with just a hint of boxers showing... There will be the Hello Kitty groups dressed in frilly pink and white dresses with frills all over, high knee socks with frills, Hello Kitty bows in their hair, Hello Kitty pins on their dresses and pulling pink Hello Kitty portable bags on wheels - quite a sight! Here kitty, kitty, kitty... nice kitty...

And Gothic, well you will do a double take. **DO** go to **Harajuku** on a Sunday and **DO** take in the atmosphere. This is one side of Tokyo that a visitor might rarely ever see.

DO walk towards **Omotesando** (away from Harajuku) and you will enter the high fashion district of Tokyo. Go on a Friday or Saturday evening, window shop, take in the couples and the general atmosphere. It is very enervating. And then make your way over to Shibuya where you will see more young crowds and shops that cater to their every whim.

And then there is Akihabara...

The name of Akihabara has become generally well known around the world as the centre for electrical appliances and electronic goods. There are large discount stores in other parts of Tokyo but in Akihabara, everything is centrally located and it is truly one-stop shopping. From the six major stores all located within a short walk from the station to the hundreds of small shops and stalls on the back and side streets, one can find just about anything - pricey stereos and computers to spy cameras to small parts and connectors and electrical parts used in construction. It is all there.

Nowadays however Akihabara has taken on another image all its own, that of a kind of anime centre. All kinds of animation videos, including soft porn, are sold here.

Akihabara also has become *otaku* or geek town. Geeks, according to one rag, have poor social ability, and have never fully matured as adults. Therefore, they are not good at communicating with others, cannot date real human beings, and instead adore an imaginary character. And Geeks even have their own pecking order, such as PC geeks, anime geeks, magazine geeks and others. Magazine geeks are geeks who have made original animation fantasy stories influenced from TV and game animation and publish them in small magazines circulated among themselves. This group are those geeks who love to play video games in which erotic animation is used. It is said that they have mush for brains and cannot distinguish between reality and their imaginary worlds. And there are coffee shops that cater to these geeks as well (**DO** see section on coffee shops). It is not cool to be considered a geek although the media are playing up this aspect of Tokyo life more and more so that in one sense it is becoming a little midstream.

INNS AND BATHS

Staying at a Japanese *Ryokan* (Inn) is a unique experience. To name this or that inn as the best or the worst is impossible. The best option is to search the web for 'Japanese Inn(s)' and a wealth of information will be available as well as tips on how to make reservations. If you have acquaintances that have travelled to Japan and have stayed at inns, **DO** talk to them to get their opinions and impressions. In this way you can make an informed decision.

Inns come in all sizes (capacities) and styles and shapes. Suffice it to say that for smaller inns you might be greeted at the front entrance by the mistress, the *kami-san*. This honoured position means that she is in charge of everything. If so greeted, **DO** remove your shoes, slip on some slippers arranged at the front entrance and follow her to check in and then to your room. If she does not meet you, then more than likely there will be someone from the staff to show you the way. This is a personalized service and is given to all guests. Rooms are Japanese style, meaning *tatami* mats and are partitioned by sliding *fusuma* screens made of thick decorative paper. If there is a small entrance to the room, **DO** leave your slippers

there and walk on the *tatami* mats in your stocking feet. If not, leave your slippers outside the door. **DON'T** worry - nobody will walk off with them. There will be simple furniture in the room with a low table in the centre. **DO** sit (on the *tatami*) at the table where tea will be prepared and served. After that the hotel person will depart and you are on your own.

Most people go to inns to relax, enjoy the surrounding area - whether in town or in the country - and to take a bath, which more than likely is a hot spring bath, or *onsen*. Guests bathe before dinner. **DO** note that in the room will be a *yukata*, which is a light cotton-like *kimono* in summer or a slightly heavier (and warmer) *kimono* in winter. Both will also have a half-coat, called a *tanzen*, appropriate to the season. **DO** remove your street clothes and put on the *yukata*. Slipping the *yukata* over you, wrap the right side first to your body and then the left side overlapping the right. While holding this in place, wrap the sash around your waist; for men who have a paunch, place it under the paunch. Then tie the sash - sometimes if a long sash, it can be wrapped twice around you - in a double knot in front and then slip the sash around so that it is at the small of your back. Then slip on the *tanzen* over the yukata. **DON'T** wrap the left side first with the right side on top - this is used only for corpses! This garb can be worn in the inn, outside or really at any time and it is quite acceptable. Now grab the small towel that is usually in the room and amble on down to the bath.

Japanese follow etiquette that the normal westerner or foreigner would not be aware of so here are the **DOs** and **DON'Ts** of the bath. However let us say right here that with some exceptions (**DO** read on) there is separated bathing. Mixed

bathing is not the norm in 2006. Some inns have several pools at different temperatures for those wishing to experience a slightly 'cooler' bath although it may be considered scalding to the foreigner. There are baths that are located outside (men & women separated by a screen) and these are called *rotenburo* - a truly unique and serene experience. Also some inns do have family baths but **DO** ask about this at the front desk. Hot springs all have different natural qualities, colour of water (from muddy to clear) and nutrients. Some are ballyhooed for people with arthritis or various illnesses and ailments. Needless to say for the ladies (and for the men too!) hot springs are especially kind and healthful for one's skin. So to the **DOs** and **DON'Ts**:

Prior to actually entering the bath room, **DO** place all your clothes in the baskets located in the ante-room or changing room. **DON'T** bring your valuables with you.

And with that small towel that you brought with you **DO** cover yourself appropriately. For men this is rather easy but those small towels - postage stamp size almost - will not cover the ladies. If in a dither as to what or where to cover, **DO** strategically cover your lower regions. Fellow bathers are going to look regardless of what or wherever so.....**DO** leave your modesty in your room or at home. However we should say here, that it is really best to bring an extra towel with you to dry yourself. Sometimes there are extra towels in the ante-room and sometimes not - it really depends on the inn.

You have now entered the bath room. **DON'T** immediately enter the bath. **DO** rinse your body first using the faucets that line the walls or use one of the water scoops to scoop water from the bath to rinse your body. If you wish at that time, you may wash yourself with soap also; that is acceptable but **DO** thoroughly rinse off the soap first *before* entering the bath.

DON'T wash yourself with soap in the bath. This is a **BIG** no-no!

After rinsing, and while going from the faucets, **DO** cover yourself again - strategically of course - and then enter the bath. **DO** be careful (if not used to it) it may be hotter than you think! Sink in slowly and then savour the healing waters for as long as you wish. After the first soak, go back to the faucets and wash yourself completely. Usually there are shower heads to use as well. After this you may re-enter the bath for as long as you wish. Some

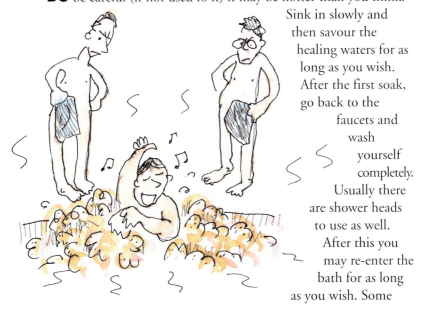

folks follow this routine a few times and get as red as a Maine lobster - parboiled! It is guaranteed you will feel like a limp rag after soaking in hot springs, that is, totally relaxed.

DON'T be raucous in the bath and **DON'T** sing loud songs and **DON'T** drink booze. **DO** take care not to disturb other bathers. Light conversation of course is allowed as groups will bathe together.

DON'T be like the Russian seamen, who put into Otaru port, a seaport in Hokkaido and who were eventually banned from using the baths because of their 'barbarian' customs. This led to 'Japanese only' signs being put up in all kinds of stores and businesses in effect barring *all* foreigners from patronizing them. The bath house and the city of Otaru were eventually sued based on racial discrimination and negligence of the Constitution and the UN Convention Against Racial Discrimination to which Japan is a signatory. It was eventually ruled that the bath house was found negligent and had to pay a fine. The city of Otaru however, was exonerated of the responsibility to follow the international treaty (UN). However the bad taste lingers to this day we are told. If the reader wishes to read more about this case, **DO** go to: http://www.debito.org/otarulawsuit.htm.

Public baths still exist in Japan although there are far fewer public baths in 2006 compared to 40 or 50 years ago. However the etiquette mentioned above also applies to the public bath as well so **DO** be careful about following this and **DON'T** be like those Russian seamen.

Having said that there is no mixed bathing, you might want to consider the *Sennin Buro*, which is mixed bathing, (or 1,000 person bath) at *Sukayu Onsen* in Aomori Prefecture. If you are shy **DON'T** go but if you want to try then **DO** so! There are several baths in the room. We are told that most bathers start with the hottest one and then gradually work down to the cooler and then finally use the shower under the bath's 'waterfalls.' After that they go back to the first or the hottest one and start the whole process over again. Sukayu Onsen Inn's phone number is 0177-38-6400 (Japanese language only).

Having finished your bath...
All meals are usually taken in the room so there is a certain amount of privacy. On the other hand be forewarned that the room maid will come and go at will to set up and serve dinner, clean up and to spread the *futon* mattress out on the *tatami* mats after you have dined. You will also be awakened in the morning and are expected to get up reasonably quickly as the room maid will then enter, fold up the futon and prepare and set out the breakfast. While dinner may consist of some specialty of the inn, the breakfast will more than likely be Japanese style which consists of rice, *miso* (bean paste) soup, possibly some fish and Japanese style pickles. Some inns may offer a more conventional western style breakfast so **DO** ask if it is available.

DO keep in mind the comings and goings of the room maid. **DON'T** be like the American couple, who having finished a full course dinner with beer and Japanese sake, were

dos & don'ts **in JAPAN**   59

starting to feel the call of love. Pushing the table and leftover dinner portions to one side, they decided to make love right there on the *tatami* mat since the *futon* had not yet been laid out. *"Gomen kudasai"* ("excuse me") the maid slightly intoned from behind the sliding door while at the same time sliding it aside. To her surprise or perhaps disbelief, there was the couple entwined in passion. The lady jumped up and off her mate to grab a robe and the poor fellow was left there lying on the mat, his ardour fully exposed. The maid quickly closed the door and silently made her way down the corridor. Checking out the next morning, slight smirks on the faces of the staff could be detected here and there. So **DO** be aware of this and keep your love making to after everything is cleaned up and the *futon* is laid out for the night.

We hope you enjoy your stay in a Japanese *Ryokan*.

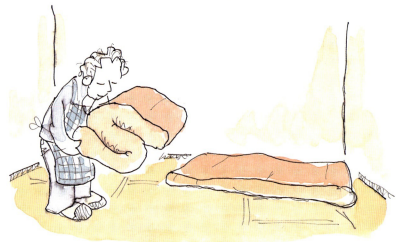

ENTERTAINMENT

There was a time many, many years ago that Tokyo was off the beaten track when it came to foreign entertainment groups. Nowadays the visitor or resident, by just picking up any copy of one of the English Language dailies prior to the weekend, will find two to three page spreads showing all that is happening in town. The *Metropolis* magazine which is free also carries public announcements that detail along with maps, what's on. This magazine also carries a huge listing along with advertisements for clubs, pubs, bars, restaurants, happy hours, events, along with directions or a small inset map. One would be hard pressed not to find anything to do on the weekend. **DO** get the paper or **DO** pick up this magazine - available in most bookstores or supermarkets and a host of other places too - and find out what suits you.

Concert halls, jazz pubs, rock events, Japan pops events, museums from classical to modern art, movie theatres, stage and drama, big domes, street events - they all have their place in Tokyo. We encourage the reader to investigate.

Movie theatres abound and they all have the latest releases but there are two theatres, Iwanami Hall (in Jinbocho) and Tokyu Bunka Mura (in Shibuya) that carry and show movies from many different countries and those not made in Hollywood. **DON'T** expect to see a Brad Pitt movie at these two locations. For the regular movie theatres however, they are to be found all over Tokyo.

There is no smoking in any theatre; it is illegal. And most folks watch the credits at the end, so sit through to the very end of the film. **DO** be aware of these two things.

TV

There are no English programs on the full range of channels. But some programs like NHK news and western movies are broadcast in English. To access these programs, there is a button on the remote control which will switch the program over to English. Cable and satellite are also available and carry all of the foreign news programs and dramas and movies.

If you do not have a reasonably good command of Japanese, most programs will bore you to death. Even if you **DO** have a reasonably good command, the programs will still probably bore you to death. There are panel shows, comedy shows (**DO** read our section on humour), documentaries, quiz shows and during the daytime, police detective shows and the *homu doramas* or home dramas, a.k.a. soaps - one after the other to satisfy the poor housewife stuck at home with the kids. The soaps in Japan are really no different from other countries, dealing as they do with cheating, love triangles, mothers-in-law (a favourite theme), wacko nerds, stalkers, *lolicon* (Lolita complex), *maza-con* (mother complex) and on and on it goes. So if you're a *loli* or *maza* kinky type person, **DO** learn some Japanese and enjoy!

Quiz shows are a curious bunch. In other countries, the average Joe or Mary will appear on quiz shows and try and make a bundle of money in winnings. In Japan, celebrities appear and compete with one another in some inane quiz and at the end of the show, the celeb gets a prize and in some cases a rather pricey one...as if they really need it.

For New Year's Eve, if you're not out with the gang, enjoy some really good music shows from about 6:00pm to midnight. The annual awards for the best singer (equivalent to a Grammy) are held and after this show NHK kicks in with its annual end-of-year four hour extravaganza of singers and dance acts, divided into the red and white teams. This used to be **THE** show to watch for many years but fortunately or unfortunately according to your viewpoint, its popularity is on the wane and so there are many other shows on the commercial channels that compete with the NHK show. But if you really like music and want to hear a good cross-section of Japanese music, from pops to traditional, then **DO** tune in.

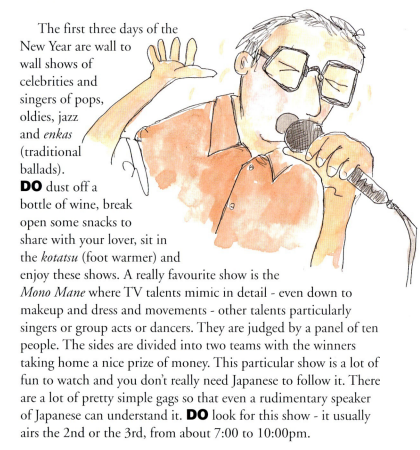

The first three days of the New Year are wall to wall shows of celebrities and singers of pops, oldies, jazz and *enkas* (traditional ballads). **DO** dust off a bottle of wine, break open some snacks to share with your lover, sit in the *kotatsu* (foot warmer) and enjoy these shows. A really favourite show is the *Mono Mane* where TV talents mimic in detail - even down to makeup and dress and movements - other talents particularly singers or group acts or dancers. They are judged by a panel of ten people. The sides are divided into two teams with the winners taking home a nice prize of money. This particular show is a lot of fun to watch and you don't really need Japanese to follow it. There are a lot of pretty simple gags so that even a rudimentary speaker of Japanese can understand it. **DO** look for this show - it usually airs the 2nd or the 3rd, from about 7:00 to 10:00pm.

During the rest of the year, sports such as baseball and soccer get aired. In the past it was a really strange thing to see the baseball game cut off at exactly 8:55pm regardless of the score or whether the game was finished or not! So it could have been the bottom of the 9th with 2 outs, the score tied and Hideki Matsui (now with the N.Y. Yankees) coming to bat and bingo, 'sorry folks we are unfortunately running out of time, tune in to your radio station to hear the rest of the game...' (no joke). However TV stations have seen the light and now air the game to its finish - most of the time.

Print Media

Japan has three English language dailies all available by subscription or at the station kiosk. There are regular columnists who write commentary on sports, life in Tokyo, the bureaucracy and off-the-beaten-track type topics. One can buy imported books at the major bookstore chains, Maruzen and Kinokuniya and a host of smaller stores. You will not lack for print and there are quite a few second hand book stores as well.

DO check a couple of websites like GaijinPot, for details on second hand bookstores. You will love the prices.

Museums

All the major museums are listed in the publications noted in the preceding paragraphs but just to mention a few of the better well known ones:

Ueno Station Area: A short walk from Ueno Station, a major juncture for train lines, the Ueno area has **The National Museum of Western Art, Tokyo Metropolitan Art Museum, Tokyo National Museum, The National Science Museum, SCAI-The Bathhouse** (not a bathhouse!) and the **Ueno Royal Museum.** All of these museums feature a wide variety or exhibitions from classical to modern. There is a standard entry fee for adults but with a cheaper fee for children and students. The exhibitions are changed regularly throughout the year.

Tokyo Station Area

Bridgestone Museum of Art: Not a museum devoted to vulcanized rubber and car tyres. A short walk from Tokyo Station, this museum features 19th century Impressionists and a permanent exhibition of artefacts from classical Rome, Greece and Egypt.

The National Museum of Art, Film Center: Nearest station is Kyobashi Station on the Ginza line. This museum exhibits film collections from well known photographers.

There are many more museums not only in the Tokyo Station area but throughout Tokyo. **DO** look in the publications previously noted.

And for those who want something a little different...
We've already mentioned elsewhere the **Meguro Parasite Museum, the Kite Museum, the Toy Museum and The Ramen Museum in Yokohama.** Here are a few others that may spark your investigative interests:

The Irish Button Museum

Are buttons your thing? This tiny museum has nothing but buttons. You can view German toggle buttons, Hungarian Turkish buttons, and an Andalusian button - your guess is as good as ours as to what that is - from the 16th century, apparently the pride of the museum. Hours are Monday through Friday, 10-12 and 1-5. Telephone: (03) 3864-6537; Admission: ¥300.

The Criminology Museum

If your interest extends to Japanese torture techniques, ninjas and other such horrors as iron maidens and guillotines, this museum located in the campus of Meiji University is for you.

dos & don'ts **in JAPAN** 67

Telephone: (03) 3296-4431. It's even more creepy than the Parasite Museum.

And while not on the list of the world's most famous museums - probably not on any list anywhere - we have:

The Laundry Museum dedicated to everything and anything connected with doing laundry. It features equipment and even irons and some paintings all to do with soapsud arts. And if that isn't enough to spark your interest there is an 8,000 volume library devoted entirely to laundry. If you want to know the best way to get that ink stain out of your jacket, or the wine stain off your little black dress, **DO** go to this one. Telephone: (03) 3759-1336.

And not forgetting...

The Rubber Baseball Museum - devoted to, well, rubber baseballs and more rubber baseballs and even more rubber baseballs. Telephone: (03) 3622-4470.

Enough about museums...

Gambling:

Casino style gambling is illegal despite the talk of the present governor of Tokyo wanting to legalize it for the city. **DON'T** hold your breath on this happening too soon though.

You may wonder what the attraction is all about concerning *pachinko* but if you like noise and smoky atmospheres, **DO** try it. You can lose yourself in the maze of lights, the whirring noises, the clanking of hundreds and thousands of metal balls rolling around in the machine and the bing-bongs of bells and music - *loud* music - and announcements, *loud* announcements made on top of the music. The metal balls that are won are exchanged for gifts or for cash at small offices close to the *pachinko* parlours. You see, legally the parlours cannot do this as that would be well...classified as gambling and as said above, gambling is illegal. So somebody else does it. There's always a loophole! Some Japanese claim to be able to live a comfortable life on their *pachinko* earnings so if you want to try this **DO** so but we hope you don't wind up a homeless person trying. However two absolute requisites are (1) one must have a strong backside and (2) lungs of steel to follow the *pachinko* way of life. We heard of one guy who got lost in the world of *pachinko* and blinking lights. Did he ever return? No he never returned and his fate is still unlearned...

Betting on horse races is legal and there are tracks all across the nation. There are special races, like the Emperor's Cup that are huge events with rather large purses. Betting is also heavy at these times; there is off-track betting available throughout Tokyo and other cities.

Recently there was one horse that never won a race in her lifetime of racing - *Haruurara* is her name and it means serene spring - not exactly a name that would inspire a winner in racing. The horse was ballyhooed in the news and on TV so people flocked to the track to bet on her in the hopes that she would win them a bundle. Sad to say the poor filly kept to her destiny and never won a race - 113 races in all and not even one win. And true to form she lost her very last outing before retirement. The track made a huge profit however when all those folks showed up to see the horse. And now there is a movie and a song and *Haruurara* goods - for good luck if you can believe it - that are now popular.

10,000,000++ to 1

The Japan Lottery Association in cooperation with the Mizuho Bank sponsor different lotteries throughout the year. There are local lotteries, 'numbers,' scratch lotteries and the main ones, the summer and year end lotteries. The grand prize for these two jumbo lotteries as they are called is ¥300,000,000 along with smaller prizes as well. There are some favourite lottery locations where people flock to, to buy the tickets as these shops carry 'special luck' since there have been a number of winners who bought there. One such place is located close to the Ginza, the first *kanji* of *gin* meaning money or gold, and people line up hours in advance on the first day of selling hoping that the luck of money will rub off on them. **DO** be aware however that the odds are enormous so your chance of winning that big one is slim. However if you do win, then **DO** a jig around the block and go out and buy some Dom Perignon because the winnings are tax free - in Japan anyway!

EATING AND DRINKING

Like any huge city, Tokyo is chock full of restaurants and the selection is infinite.

For Japanese a western style breakfast is apparently the most popular; but a truly dyed-in-the wool Japanese style breakfast might turn off a westerner. It would consist of fish, rice, miso soup, dried seaweed, pickles and more than likely *natto*, which is fermented soybean. It is best said that *natto* is an acquired taste. It looks OK but it smells and tastes, well, different and it is sticky and leaves a sticky taste in your mouth. As you pick it up, it makes a little spider web and you have to wave your chopsticks in a circle to get rid of the long threads that it makes.

One can eat quite reasonably for lunch as most restaurants have set lunchtime menus and the quantity is quite sufficient. Most major office buildings have a restaurant floor at the B1 or B2 level. As they fill up quickly from noon, **DO** get there early but **DON'T** linger either as once finished, you are expected to leave.

Japan has been invaded once again but this time it is all of those fast food chains that one can find anywhere. If that is your choice, you won't lack even in the least little bit. However statistics show that Japanese are gradually getting fatter - not as bad as Americans though - as the western style diet takes more and more precedence over the traditional Japanese diet. *Sashimi* or raw fish is

now more expensive than beef and foods made from grains like wheat, also comprise a large part of the diet.

The most popular type of food is *ramen* or Chinese style noodles. There is nothing more heavenly that a steaming bowl of *ramen* on a cold winter day. And there are cold noodles as well in the summer. The varieties are endless. **DO** try this unique food.

A quick check of a local convenience store has 75 - yes 75 - (counted by the author himself) different kinds of instant noodles.

Soba which is made from buckwheat is also popular and there are soba stands near every train station. You'll see a lot of office people downing their bowl of *soba* in the morning. And try *tentama soba* or *soba* with a raw egg - it'll cure your hangover!

Some reminders:

Is the place open or closed? If there is *noren* or a horizontal shop curtain on a pole outside the front door, then it is open, if hanging on the inside, then it is closed.

Some restaurants will offer an *oshibori* or hot towel before dinner. **DO** use it to wipe your hands and face but **DON'T** take a bath with it or blow your nose in it. **DON'T** be like the westerner who used it to wash his armpits on a hot summer's day either. If in a *sushi* restaurant, you may keep it by your plate to wipe your fingers occasionally.

Rice always comes with the meal. In traditional restaurants several courses may be served with rice appearing last as it is considered the staple of the meal.

DO try to learn how to use chopsticks. Western-style restaurants will of course set a knife and fork out but for most places chopsticks are the order of the day. And those noodle or *soba* places only have chopsticks. However **DON'T** jab at the rice with your chopsticks and **DON'T** 'stand them up' in the rice bowl either - that is how it is done when making an offering at a deceased person's grave or altar.

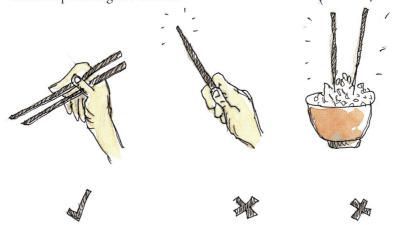

DON'T use your chopsticks to point at anybody - it's very impolite.

If transferring food from one plate to another, **DON'T** use the 'mouth' end of your chopsticks but **DO** invert them to pick up the food.

There are a lot of chopstick taboos. Many people do a lot of these no-no's at an informal meal but it's good to know that they're not accepted behaviour everywhere so you can avoid them in genteel company or when you want to make a good impression. Most of them are self-evident. So **DON'T**:

- touch one piece of food with your chopsticks and then decide on another one.
- push food around looking for your favourite.
- move your chopsticks around several dishes in indecision.
- hold your chopsticks with a fist.
- touch your food with your chopsticks and then put them down without eating it.
- ask for *okawari* (seconds) while holding your chopsticks.
- pierce or stab your food with your chopsticks.
- let soup drip from your chopsticks.
- lick your chopsticks like some old geezer.
- pick up something with your chopsticks closed, like using a spoon.
- put your mouth to the side of a dish and use the chops to shovel the food into your mouth. Kids may do this and it would be accepted however.
- clink the tableware with your chopsticks.
- place your chopsticks across a dish or bowl like a bridge.
- pull a dish towards yourself with your chopsticks.

And a BIG **DON'T**.....**DON'T** pass food using your chopsticks to another. This particular no-no originates from the practice after the cremation of picking up the remaining bones and together with another, placing a bone or piece of bone into the urn.

And **DO** learn the etiquette for using toothpicks. **DON'T** chomp on it and then spit it out like some uncouth lout, or let it dangle from your mouth like a cigarette. While using the toothpick, cover your mouth with the other hand and when finished, set it down. **DON'T** use it to pick your nose or your ears either.

It is quite OK to slurp your noodles or *soba* so **DO** slurp away and **DON'T** be put off by others who do the same. Same goes for soup - raise the bowl and drink from the bowl directly and slurp if you feel like it.

Except for hotel or other major restaurants, cash is used at most places so **DON'T** expect to use credit cards at most restaurants or drinking places and of course, yen only.

There is no custom of tipping in Japan - anyplace - so **DON'T** be concerned about it. Only in hotels or upscale restaurants will a service charge be added.

A lot of small places have plastic food displays outside - they look so good like they could be eaten. So if you can't speak the language, just point to the display. If you want to buy one of those plastic displays, there is a section of Tokyo that sells them exclusively. They are rather expensive though.

You will find that if you go to a drinking place, the food dishes are small and so it is expected that you will order three or four of them to go with your drinks. So just point to what looks good or what the master is making behind the counter.

Hmmm......you see a place that looks interesting. There's no plastic display, no English signs and probably nobody speaks English either. You want to go; you break out in a cold sweat. Do you let your nerves get the best of you and move on to a place that's safe or do you give in to your adventurous side? To many visitors or foreign residents, lack of language skills can pose a formidable barrier to enjoying the culinary delights of Japan. So what to do?

Here are some **TIPS:**

1. Look around. What part of town are you in? Does it seem garish or are there lots of business people? If you see plenty of suits **DO** feel at ease. These folks will usually congregate in moderately priced places.

2. If you're in a garish part of the city **DON'T** go in unless accompanied by a Japanese acquaintance.

3. **DO** take a look at the menu to see if there are prices. If no prices **DO** be wary. You'll be setting yourself up for 'sticker shock' when you get the bill. If all seems OK however, just point or if you see something on another table, point to that.

4. Business people? **DO** try and strike up a conversation. Most business folks have a basic use of English and would more than likely be willing to help. When these folks get to drinking and they spy a foreigner, you just might be asked to join them for a drink or two. So **DO** take up their invitation but **DON'T** expect to have a conversation in English about Prime Minister Shinzo Abe's cabinet choices or the relations between Japan and China.

5. **DON'T** go into any place that has touts outside. These places are usually clubs and the meters start running when you sit down with a host or hostess. So unless you have umpteen jillions of yen in some offshore banking account or you are with somebody that has an unlimited expense account, **DON'T** go in.

6. **DON'T** be put off by places that have No Foreigners Allowed signs. **DO** ignore them and go someplace else and besides who needs the aggravation anyway?

Drinking places and such, Bars, Snacks, *Izakaya's* Host/hostess bars

Traditionally and historically, alcohol is the lubricant that puts oil on the wheels of relationships and friendships. It has always been part and parcel of the society and Japanese also use it to let their hair down and talk about things that they might not necessarily talk about on other occasions. And the more alcohol one drinks, the looser the tongue becomes.

DO wait for your glass to be filled and **DO** wait for the *kanpai* (cheers) when all will raise their glasses together. And **DO** offer to refill others' glasses as well as have your own filled. It is considered impolite to pour your own drink when drinking from a common bottle such as beer or sake. Individual cocktails are another matter however and these can be drunk at one's own pace. **DO** understand that Japanese may want to engage you in a drinking contest and the more the merrier and the happier one gets, the better the atmosphere. After all that's what going to a drinking place is all about.

DO order several dishes as they will be small. There are places that specialize in certain food such as *yakitori* (grilled chicken) so the menu will mainly be comprised of chicken parts - all parts - that are grilled plus other side dishes such as vegetables or *tofu* or the like. Everybody partakes so **DO** put a little of each onto your own plate.

There are lots of little stand bars near train stations and you'll see lots of salaried people having 'one for the road' before they board the train. Even in these places, it is expected that the customer will order something to eat, even if it's only peanuts.

A great side dish in summer is *eda-mame* or boiled soybeans which are then served cold. **DON'T** eat the whole bean - only the beans inside - very popular and healthy too. After all you gotta have something with all that alcohol.

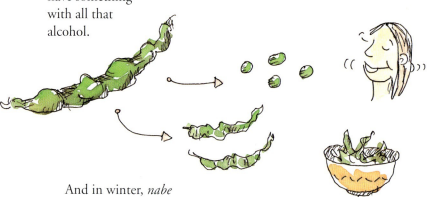

And in winter, *nabe* dishes with meats or vegetables cooked in a communal earthenware pot on a portable stove is just great - that and some sake and you will sleep soundly that night.

In Fukuoka city (Kyushu) there are *yattai* or outdoor wagon carts, actually *stationary* outdoor wagon carts. Other cities have them too but Fukuoka is famous for them. In summer they are open but in winter tarps are hung from the sides to block out the cold. These are cheap and the food is fresh and wholesome and there is nothing like a cold beer in summer after a day's work to wash away all the trials and tribulations of the office. **DO** put away your nervousness if in Fukuoka and try out the *yattai*.

To address host and hostess bars briefly, **DO** realize that you will be paying top price if a host or hostess sits with you. All prices are inflated. The hosts/hostesses are ranked according to their 'sales' in one month. **DO** understand that you will be encouraged to drink, drink, drink and order high priced snacks for the pleasure of their company. Some places are rip-offs with the owner or 'custodians' being associated with certain elements of society and they are not immune to using threats or promising bodily harm if you as the customer balk at the total bill. **DO** beware of these types of places.

In addition to Walkmans and Hondas and hybrid cars, what is the other invention from Japan that is known around the world? Karaoke of course! Karaoke rooms and studios abound in Japan and rooms can be rented by the hour with drinks and snacks extra. So if invited, **DO** go for the experience - even if you don't sound like Elvis or Mariah and **DO** sing *My Way*, one of the most popular English - and probably the only one as well - songs on the karaoke menu.

Restaurants in general: inviting and being invited

A lot to be said about this topic is really common sense but some general pointers.

DO ask your host about the menu and what is good or what is recommended. Some restaurants have a special for the day or if seafood, a special catch for the day.

If a Chinese style restaurant, **DO** read *The **DOs** and **DON'Ts** in our Hong Kong* book. They apply as well in Japan.

DO follow the etiquette concerning the first drink as mentioned above.

For hotel restaurants, service charge and tax are added to the bill. For all other types of restaurants, the tax is usually included in the total.

If you're the invitee, **DO** expect that your host will settle the bill.

At the start of the meal, **DO** say *"itadakimasu"* and at the end *"gochisosama deshita."*

DO pay the bill at the cash register; it is not customary to give the payment to waiters/waitresses.

Coffee/Café Shops

Sometimes we think that the Japanese invented the coffee shop. If you need to kill time or you want to have a different kind of experience - **DO** read on - then try out a cafe. Tokyo has six or seven (as of last count) main chain store cafés and they are everywhere. While most have both smoking and non-smoking sections, there are still a couple that have all smoking. **DO** check at the counter if this is a concern.

So there are jazz cafés, classic music cafés, singing cafés, *manga* cafes, gallery cafés, Japanese tea cafés, maid cafés, oxygen cafés, reptile cafés, antique cafés, impossibly expensive cafés ... you can just open your dictionary and attach 'café' to the first word you see and the Japanese probably have it.

Here are some examples:

Maid cafés - This is one of the latest breeds; the waitresses are dressed like handmaids and we are told they exist in obscure byways of Akihabara, and are loyally patronized by the *Otaku* (geeks) that inhabit the town. There's nothing obscene about them and men who visit them with erotic fantasies in their heads will often be disappointed and wonder what the fuss is all about. They're just regular cafés, except that the girls wear costumes and call you ... well, *"goshujin-sama"* (an honorific term). But for the *Otaku*, it is the ultimate paradise, the Shangri-la.

Meikyoku kissa, or Classical Music Cafés — Along with the Jazz *kissa*, this is a disappearing breed, but some still stubbornly hang on here and there. These are cafés with tens and thousands of classical music records (not CDs but always LPs - and some even have the old '45' records!) on their shelves which they play regularly in large volume. Their record collections usually stop somewhere in the mid-Sixties, and because they are played over and over again, the acoustics are themselves 'classical' as well. Often they will accept requests from the customers. Conversation is either prohibited, or kept at a whispering level. The coffee is usually disgusting. Usually they have these Gothic interiors full of antiques, silent clocks, broken dolls, real cobwebs, and the owner looks like he/she is allergic to sunlight. You feel as if time has actually stopped in the place a long, long time ago.

Manga kissa - these are ubiquitous today - near every station, near every junction, look around for the word "マンガ" among the buildings and you'll find one - or two or three, usually - up in some sixth or seventh floor of a dirty building. Nowadays they also provide internet connection, DVD players, play station, and free drinks. The seats are arranged in private booths for one or for couples, with a PC and game console in each. Around the walls and in between the booths are the rows of bookshelves, or the *manga*-shelves, that house tens of thousands of that entertainment. People are charged by the length of their stay and any other extra services they may use, such as snacks (everything from potato chips to macaroni gratin), or rented external PC devices. The fees are usually something like ¥450 for the first hour, and then ¥70 every 10 minutes. The idea is to make patrons stay longer so the free games, the *manga*, DVD's, reclining seats, headphones, meal delivery, private and windowless booths are all part of the design to make you pay for that extra 10 minutes to finish another book, or clear another stage in a video game. But since they're usually open 24 hours, they're handy for those nights when you missed the last train, and need a cheap place to wait for the morning train - they often offer 'night packs' like ¥1,200 for 5 hours especially for those kinds of guests.

No-pan kissa - these were extremely popular 10 to 15 years ago and you can still find a few here and there. *No-pan* is 'no panties' in English and the 'waitresses' - for lack of a better word - will wait on your table wearing a very short, short skirt - we must keep our modesty of course - and well... nothing underneath. For those who wish to be titillated, try it out. Prices are fixed but no touching please!

Couples kissa (cafés) for well... couples only. It would be weird if you went in alone, so **DON'T**. Prices are by the hour. Technically speaking, the price is for the cup of coffee or drink but in reality the couple basically rents a private space - and these come in all kinds of motif - and is free to do whatever they wish. We will leave the rest up to your imagination.

And in Nagoya, we understand that the competition for customers is quite cutthroat. With your cuppa in the morning, you will be served some kind of snack to go with it. Peanuts seem to be a popular item. Peanuts and coffee? Well only in Japan.

In Osaka, there is the famous *Dotonbori* area for eating. This area is known as *kuidaore machi* - or eating yourself silly to the point of squandering your money - and Osakans love to eat and joke and have fun - more so than others from different cities. One of the most popular foods in Osaka is *takoyaki* or round breaded octopus dumplings.

Tired of all this restaurant and bar talk?

Well you can stay home and order a PIZZA! There are the usual pizza chain stores found everywhere but in one pizza shop someplace in Tokyo (we're not saying) you can have...

Seafood Special Pizza with shrimp, squid, octopus, clams, scallops and crab legs. We think we'll go for a swim in the ocean.

Garlic Steak Pizza comes with cubed beef, garlic and seasoned with steak sauce. DON'T ask your girlfriend out after you have one of these! Or maybe your wife will probably ask you (or maybe tell you) to sleep in the next room.

Japanese Style Pizza is scrumptious with toppings of shredded pork, *shimeji* mushrooms, bamboo shoots, seaweed and perilla leaves. Mmmmmmm good!

And a favourite for those people who **DON'T** want to lose weight. **The Idaho Special** with potatoes (from Idaho naturally!) topped with gobs and gobs of mayonnaise. Yeah cholesterol city!

And the favourite of all times.....
Squid Ink Pizza. Instead of tomato sauce, squid ink - ***black squid ink*** - is used as the basic ingredient of this pizza. One small problem though - it stains your mouth and teeth - temporarily of course. We hope you don't have a date with a photographer after eating one of these babies.

And in winter there is the *yakimo* (baked potatoes) man who may prowl your neighbourhood in a small truck playing a tape that sings endlessly, *"yakimo, yakimo, oishii yakimo desuyo."* It is a sound of winter. Be careful though, the potatoes are piping hot (they are baked in a barrel-full of heated stones) - so **DON'T** burn your mouth.

Want some quick snacks with your drinks? **DO** go to the *konbini* or convenience store - like the vending machines, they're everywhere. Just as a sampling you can get snacks like chips, *osembe* (rice crackers), peanuts, etc. but for the gourmet in you, there are also the following: dried squid, octopus, salmon chunks, sardines, just to name a few. Enjoy!

No eating section would be complete without touching on the subject of *fugu* or blowfish. Much is written about this often maligned fish. First its shape is rather grotesque and its meat tough. Chefs must have a special license in order to prepare it, especially the sashimi. The chef learns to cut the meat paper thin because of its toughness. That is why photos of *fugu* presentations show the *sashimi* laid out on a flower motif plate. The *sashimi* is so thin that the flower design is seen through it thereby lending a certain aura to the dish. The other reason that chefs must have that license is because the ovaries and liver of the *fugu* are poisonous!

Fugu liver is poisonous and it's illegal to serve, but it has a cult following and worshipers who claim that its taste, along with the indescribable sensation caused by the poison temporarily paralyzing the tongue, places it above all other delicacies. No doubt there's a Russian roulette appeal here. **DON'T** be like Mr. Mitsugoro Bando, VIII (a kabuki actor) who died in Kyoto in

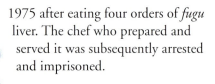

1975 after eating four orders of *fugu* liver. The chef who prepared and served it was subsequently arrested and imprisoned.

Recently a group of scholars claimed that they discovered a way to produce 'safe' *fugu* by raising them in a controlled and cultured environment. They claim that the *fugu's* poison is not produced internally but derives from their diet of certain shellfish and that by carefully controlling its feed they can make the fish poison-free. They're appealing to the government to lift the ban on eating liver produced by their method but apparently with no success. Perhaps the purists would object too because it would take away the death-cheating fun.

> *So how do you tell a fugu restaurant from other restaurants? The fugu lantern that is hung outside is an exact replica of the fish and is made from real fugu hide.*

We leave you with two proverbs about *fugu*.

It's unwise to eat *fugu* [because it's poisonous] and unwise not to [because it's delicious].

Wanting to eat *fugu* but scared of dying. (Used to express a dilemma).

CHARACTERISTICS AND TRAITS

Family & Children

Traditionally, families are close knit despite the fact that nowadays children move to the city for employment and therefore live apart from their parents. Many small towns - particularly in the agricultural sector - have experienced this phenomenon and so bemoan the fact that there are no children to carry on after them. However one's first obligation and duty are after all to one's own family members and these ties do remain quite strong, despite distances between relatives.

Children are fawned over in many, many ways and the worst offender is *obaachan* or grandma. It is not an uncommon site to see a passenger giving up his/her seat for grandma along with her grandchild  and then grandma sits the child down on the seat while she continues to stand. However the concept of *amae* or dependence is fostered from early on and continues into adult-hood of the child. Westerners are often heard to remark at how badly behaved Japanese children are and the reluctance of parents to scold their offspring in public. Just recently a motorman let his child into the driver's cab of a train because the child (with his mother) started screaming for his father when he found out his dad was the driver. The poor motorman is now likely to lose his job for breaking company rules. The outpouring of opinions in the papers all sided with Dad however, pleading with the company hierarchy to show mercy to poor Papa for allowing his son into the cab.

Schools

It is generally agreed that one of the most valuable and far reaching reforms of General MacArthur was the establishment of an educational system after WWII. Prior to the war, the system was elitist but due to his reforms, it became more egalitarian and the system of "6-3-3" (primary - middle - high schools) was set up. School used to be held on Saturdays but this was dropped a few years ago. **DON'T** be surprised to see kids loaded down with a book bag on their backs, a cloth bag filled with other things for class and perhaps a soccer ball or musical instrument on the other arm. Copious amounts of homework are given even during summer and winter breaks. For public schools, kids wear their own clothes and yellow caps - for traffic safety - but private school kids wear school uniforms. One of the cutest things is to see all the boys and girls dressed in their uniforms, walking to school in the morning.

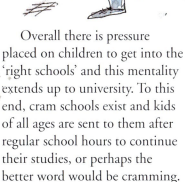

Overall there is pressure placed on children to get into the 'right schools' and this mentality extends up to university. To this end, cram schools exist and kids of all ages are sent to them after regular school hours to continue their studies, or perhaps the better word would be cramming.

In days past, the university entrance exams were known as 'entrance examination hell' due to the fierce pressure and competition on trying to get into that name university. This has eased a little bit because universities are experiencing increasingly empty classrooms. Due to the falling birth rate they're loosening up their entrance requirements in a bid to keep classrooms filled.

To acquaint you with Japan and the Japanese themselves we will touch on some characteristics of the people.

Names

When addressing Japanese, the suffix *san* is always used, so for example, Tanaka-*san*. When Japanese speak to each other, they will use the surname as opposed to the pronoun "you." So **DO** use this suffix. *Chan* however is used when addressing children or it will also be used among family members or close life-long friends. However as the foreigner, **DO** avoid using *chan* if you're unsure of its usage. *Sama* is the very polite form of *san* but is usually used in the addressee of a formal letter.

Tate Shake or Vertical Society

This phrase coined by author Nakane Chie accurately reflects the feudalistic nature of Japanese society as established in the 16th and 17th centuries with different classes of people from the samurai at the top down to the lowly outcasts, the tanners and gravediggers. This trait emphasizes the group-think for which Japan is famous with each class fostering a sense of belonging to one group or the other and even a ranking from superior to inferior within that group. This trait has contributed to the characteristic of trying to keep up with the Joneses, with people paying top price for brand name goods and other luxury items.

Face

Face is an all-governing characteristic. Loss of face will engender feelings of hostility, back biting and possible revenge. In other words, lots of negative emotions. A loss of face to one's peers or within one's group or among family members entails a loss of respect. On the other hand saving face maintains that status or position and is the cement that binds one to the group. The concept and characteristic of face is so pervasive that language, culture and customs are all intricately intertwined. This means that confrontation or even a hint of confrontation is avoided in order to preserve harmonious relationships. **DO** keep this in mind when dealing with colleagues or friends or even your neighbours and **DON'T** argue points for the sake of debate. **DO** be respectful at all times.

All this of course affects language and how it is presented. So from a subordinate to a superior or elder, honorifics are used in Japanese. Japanese **DO** generally avoid saying "you" and rely on context instead; and although there are several forms of the pronoun "I" this too is generally avoided.

Skikata Ga Nai or it can't be helped

This phrase is equivalent to "what will be, will be," and it does colour the Japanese psyche in many ways. Sometimes it is used to cover a lot of sins. For example, if a politician is found to have engaged in some under the table activity, people will say, *shikata ga nai*, since that is what politicians will do and in some ways are expected to do. Or, if there is a kid misbehaving or screaming loudly on the train, people will think, "well it can be helped, it's just a kid." So in a way this phrase goes a long way to accepting what is and a realization as to what can or cannot be changed. It is a very useful phrase but one which also gives insight into the Japanese psyche.

Gaman

The word *gaman* can be used to convey, patience, perseverance, self control, endurance etc. "Patience is a virtue" goes the old saw. Japanese are brought up from early age with the concept of *gaman*. In olden days young boys wore short pants to school even in winter. This was to teach them to be impervious to the cold (*gaman*). Nowadays however, you will see them in their Nike's and designer jeans.

If you have a noisy dog in the neighbourhood - quite common these days - everybody will more than likely just put up (*gaman*) with the noise. After all raising a ruckus about it may cause a loss of face on either side - quite the opposite in western countries!

Employees routinely work late - or more accurately will stay until the boss leaves - regardless of whether they have any actual work or not. So the kid could be running a fever and the wife needs some help at home but Papa will stay in the office and subjugate (*gaman*) his own wishes or feelings to return home. However this *gaman* makes the Japanese tough competitors as they see it as a source of strength. So no matter how difficult or hard things become, they just hang in there and keep on fighting (*ganbaru*) and these traits carry the day eventually. Look how Japan recovered from the devastation of WWII. These are definitely traits to be admired. But the negative side is that people can become so blind to the reality of the situation - see the present day economy and the need for structural changes - that nothing is done (*shikata ga nai*).

Inscrutability

Just sit in on any company meeting and you will notice a group of impassive faces as the CEO or President is speaking. Not only is this due to deference of his higher status but also to the trait of inscrutability. Ride any train and see a bunch of impassive faces or people burying their noses in a book or a cell phone.

There could be mayhem happening just a few meters away but most people will remain passive. Japanese in general do not necessarily show their true feelings or emotions in front of others. This, to make a general statement, is due to inscrutability and also to a certain degree not wanting to become involved. However, after drinks in the company of colleagues, the facade is dropped and bosses will be roasted - 'well done' sometimes - and drawn and quartered. When in the private company of family or friends, Japanese are just as lively and expressive as anybody else. So **DON'T** be surprised if the subway car you are on is really quiet but **DO** prepare yourself for some lively banter and conversation at an *izakaya*, a drinking place.

Honne & Tatemae

There is the way things are and the way we'd like them to be; the reality and the facade; the substance and the form; being direct or being diplomatic. In short, that is *honne* and *tatemae*, respectively. Avoiding conflict and trouble is extremely important in Japan, so diplomatic language is often used rather than the direct approach. In formal situations, a direct "no" is usually avoided and usually a more vague answer is used. This trait is sometimes called deceptive, but it is actually a good example of how the culture and language are intertwined. Westerners may judge *tatemae* to be only a facade but the Japanese have elevated it into an art. So

a part of *tatemae* is speaking diplomatically. Instead of a "no," people may say, *"chotto muzukashii"* which is translated as "that's a little difficult" but in reality it means "**no, no way!!**"

But regardless of *honne* and *tatemae*, when it comes to logical reasoning the Japanese sometimes seem to have forgotten their brains somewhere. You will just scratch your head when you hear that ski equipment from foreign countries is unsuitable for Japan because "Japanese snow is different." Or that Japanese cannot properly digest western imported beef due to the length of their intestines. So the *honne* and *tatemae* trait tends to stress the harmony of a situation but in reality what may lie beneath might be entirely different. However this does seem to be changing a little as more and more Japanese companies work to survive in the global economy. They are finding that they have to be more up front and perhaps more aggressive in their dealings with foreign companies.

Haji or Shame

While slightly different from face, shame is in fact closely connected to it. If one brings shame upon one's family or group, then loss of face results. So avoidance of shame is an invisible force or restraint that can govern one's actions. Arguing with one's neighbour; small kids failing to get into that elite kindergarten; high school students failing university entrance exams; the salaried person committing a grievous error resulting in the company's dirty laundry being aired in public - and the list goes on and on. So a person's actions in public can be governed by the thin gossamer threads of shame that are attached to each individual.

A good example of this was the recent 'scandal' involving a high school baseball tournament when one school's team members were caught - horrors of all horrors - smoking (under 20 years is technically illegal) and the team was pulled from the tournament. There was lots of shame and embarrassment and apologizing going around for a couple of months.

Loyalty to the group or Thee & Me

Japanese society is a very close knit society. The *shimaguni* - island mentality - exists even to this day. Despite the phrases that one routinely hears - globalism or internationalism or cultural and global world - Japanese society in many aspects still retains the *shimaguni* mentality which in turn reinforces loyalty to one's group. Japanese love to show off and talk about the homogeneity of their society while blithely ignoring many of the other racial groups that are found from Hokkaido to Okinawa. The average salaryman, when speaking of or thinking about his personal relationship to others, will speak of these relationships, first to his company, then his department, then section and after that his immediate colleagues and then finally to his own individuality.

If you look at the politics of the government, the word factions is used. So and so belongs to such a faction and the Diet (governing body) is made up of many different factions all loyal to the leader of that faction. The factions make up different political parties. Needless to say this can be cumbersome at times and also can involve a lot of back scratching to get legislation passed and enacted.

This characteristic of loyalty to one's group is found at all levels of society. So as a foreigner **DON'T** be put off by this. If as a businessperson you do get the understanding and support of the group (the company) then you will get your contract or that big order.

It is also difficult for foreigners to be accepted as part of the group. The very word used for foreigner is *gaikokujin* (*gaijin* for short) or literally 'outsider.' So **DON'T** be too dismayed if people do not totally accept you. And **DON'T** become offended at indifference or disinterest shown by group members to those not part of the group. However this also extends to the Japanese themselves in that they may not accept others totally if they're not part of their own group. A good example of this is the *chonaikai* (neighbourhood group). The people in the group are friendly with each other but if you happen to live on the other side of the street and belong to a different *chonaikai* then more than likely friendly greetings will not be exchanged. So while some people see Japanese as xenophobic, they are probably attracted to cliques more than they are repelled by foreigners.

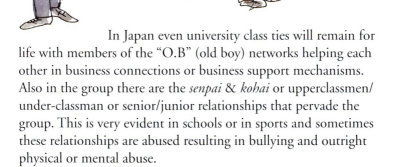

In Japan even university class ties will remain for life with members of the "O.B" (old boy) networks helping each other in business connections or business support mechanisms. Also in the group there are the *senpai* & *kohai* or upperclassmen/under-classman or senior/junior relationships that pervade the group. This is very evident in schools or in sports and sometimes these relationships are abused resulting in bullying and outright physical or mental abuse.

The *ware ware Nihonjin* ('we Japanese') expression typifies this characteristic so accurately. It colours everything as Japanese look out at the world. A perfect example of this is the highly restrictive immigration policies of the government. This thinking also explains why Japanese media will focus on the two Japanese fatalities of a plane crash while blithely ignoring the 300 people who were killed.

There are many mavericks and lone wolves in Japan however. Witness some of the famous artists and current businessmen who have gone against the social force of the group mentality and have ploughed their own ground so to speak. A good example of this is the last Prime Minister who went against the ingrained policies and O.B. networks of the Liberal Democratic Party to forge his own policies. Koizumi did head his own faction however.

In a crowd

In Tokyo people are rather impatient. This is not necessarily a lack of consideration of others but more due to the hectic pace of the city. So, **DON'T** be surprised if people push the 'door close' button on elevators. Japanese cannot wait that extra second for the door to close automatically.

DON'T become annoyed if people cut in front of you either while walking or driving.

DO be careful when driving and you come to a four way stop sign. **DON'T** expect the other car to wait for you even if you get there first.

Also **DO** watch out at traffic lights as well. Drivers routinely run the yellow light just as it turns red.

And on Tokyo's narrow back streets, **DO** pay extra attention as people will usually drive right down the middle and then swerve over to their side when another vehicle approaches.

In Tokyo **DO** stand to the left on escalators to allow those in a hurry to pass on the right. In Kansai however, stand to the right.

DO arrive early for meetings of any kind. In Okinawa however, there is 'Okinawa time' that is more relaxed and which reflects that island's unhurried atmosphere and approach to life and pace of living.

Although it is a little more common, Japanese don't eat or drink while walking or riding public transport. About the only exception to this may be kids. So **DO** follow this custom.

Cell phone use - in the Kanto area (Tokyo and its environs), **DO** put your cell phone on 'manner mode' (quiet mode) when riding public transport. Announcements to this effect are constantly made to remind people. In Kansai however, it is more acceptable to use your phone on public transport or while walking. This is said to be due to the fact that Osakans are more gregarious and so will not hesitate to make and receive calls.

Smoking - smoking while walking is now being vigorously discouraged and there are certain areas that have banned it altogether. **DO** keep this rule since you may be cautioned by volunteers of the local ward office who lurk on street corners looking for violators. For those who **DO** need to have a quick nicotine fix, there are smoking 'cars' or vans placed strategically here and there where one can drop in and have a quick smoke and then be on one's way.

Japanese do not engage in PDA's or public displays of affection. You will very seldom see people kissing or hugging in public although hand holding is prevalent. So this is another one of those customs that you should follow as heads will turn in your direction. **DON'T** be like the young couple seen in a station necking during rush hour; all heads and eyes were turned in their direction and an occasional "tsk-tsk" could be heard as well. However, all the sex crazed salaried men were risking severe neck trauma as they craned their necks to watch the spectacle (and secretly enjoy it) as the train pulled out of the station.

Overheard on a subway in the morning, "hmmm they don't seem to be too happy..." The speaker was a foreigner and he was commenting on his fellow passengers. We'll put that down to inscrutability and more than likely half of the passengers were asleep! So having read all of the foregoing, you may think that folks here have no sense of humour. On the contrary. However, what tickles people's funny bones is vastly different from western humour.

Just watch TV and you will see people being hit on the head, being dragged through snow and ice in their briefs, jumping into scalding hot water to see how long one can endure the heat, groups literally falling all over themselves or maybe into a huge vat of talcum powder or being hit in the face with huge pies and then being called *baka* (stupid) in a loud voice. And the audience is rolling in the aisles! If you ever saw the Three Stooges comedy act in the USA and their brand of slapstick comedy, then this is comparable to comedy in Japan - at least on present day TV.

There is also an equivalent of ethnic or anecdotal comedy called *rakugo* but this is a highly skilled art and learned over many years by accomplished story tellers. There are stand up comedy acts too, known as *manzai* where both comedians (one being the foil) tell humorous stories but also with a lot of head slapping or falling down and overdone actions. However Japanese don't necessarily have interactions of telling jokes with others like, "hey did you hear this one about…"

Some other traits or characteristics or customs

DO avoid excessive physical and eye contact - Japanese may stare at you the foreigner however. **DON'T** back slap or prod or point to someone with one finger - **DO** use an open hand if pointing. Also **DON'T** shout loudly or wave at someone to get his or her attention.

DO avoid chewing gum when working or in other formal situations.

DON'T wear lots of jewellery or very colourful clothes when going to work. The plain, simple dark suit, or skirt or blouse will do just fine.

DON'T scream about why nobody speaks English or why there aren't five different varieties of a product you want. Instead we recommend that you **DO** learn some basic Japanese.

DO carry a packet of tissues with you at all times. Japanese do not use handkerchiefs, that is, to blow their noses. Tissues are the norm so if you have to blow your nose, **DO** leave the room if possible, or at the very least try to turn away from other people while using a tissue. When you stop and think about it, the idea of using a handkerchief and then stuffing it back in your pocket is well… kind of yucky!

So what purpose do handkerchiefs serve? They are used to wipe one's hands after using the restroom. You see, restrooms in general - except possibly office buildings - almost never have paper towels so the handkerchief serves this purpose. So in addition to that packet of tissues, **DO** carry a handkerchief or hanky (for the ladies) too. **DON'T** be like the foreigner who, lacking a handkerchief, wiped his hands on his socks and then smoothed out his hair with still damp hands after using the bathroom.

And speaking of bodily fluids, **DON'T** be surprised if someone sneezes or coughs in your face - yep, right in your keester and with full magnum force too! While more and more folks are wearing facial masks and seem to be more aware of sneezing when they have a cold or during hay fever season, lots of folks just seem to enjoy spraying their sneezes and droplets all over the place and especially on crowded trains.

Wearing masks is quite common to guard against colds and influenza and during hay fever season. However **DON'T** be like the Japanese gentleman, while on a visit to San Francisco and wanting to change some money, walked into a bank with his mask on. Guns were drawn in a flash, the alarm went off and the cops arrived with minutes.

And continuing onto the subject of other bodily fluids and functions...lots of homes nowadays have warmed toilet seats and what are known as washlets. These contraptions not only warm your butt, but upon finishing your tinkle or more, will wash your nether regions as you wish. Some of them also come equipped with dryers so that you need not use toilet paper to wipe off the water. Most hotels have these installed in their rooms - so **DO** get ready to rock 'n roll when you sit on one with lights flashing, water spraying and hot air on your butt...or other places...

DO understand that not all places, like public toilets, have 'thrones'. There are still many squat toilets in use. In one sense these are clean in that no part of your nether regions touches anything but **DO** aim carefully (both men and women) and **DO** remove anything like cell phones from shirt pockets, otherwise it may be bye-bye to the phone as you bend over to get into position.

Japan has no tradition of making sarcastic remarks to make a point, so **DON'T** boo or use 'the finger.'

When Japanese gesture to themselves they point to their nose and not their chest.

The Japanese gesture for "come here" is to extend your hand palm facing down and raise and lower your fingers a few times. The western gesture of palm facing up is only used to call animals.

The Japanese gesture for "no" or "no thank you" is fanning your hand sideways a few times in front of your face.

It's polite to initially refuse someone's offer of help. Japanese may also initially refuse your offer even if they really want it. Traditionally an offer is made three times. It may be better to say you'll carry their bag, call a taxi, etc., instead of pushing them to be polite and refuse.

When they laugh, Japanese women often cover their mouth with their hand. It is not necessary for westerners to follow this custom but **DO** be aware of it.

This is not a custom but **DO** note how many women in Japan are pigeon toed. While out walking you may see the most beautiful of women elegantly dressed but as she walks, one foot is turned inward. **DO** sit on any train and look at the high school girls and count how many of them are pigeon toed. This is said to

come from childhood when girls are taught to sit on their legs with the feet turned in to each other and then the muscles become naturally formed to that position.

And on the subject of feet, walk in any crowd and **DO** listen to the shuffle of feet. It seems as if all of Tokyo is shuffling to some beat that only those doing it can hear. This characteristic comes from early childhood and the Japanese slippers - one size fits - that people wear and well, they shuffle around the house and the back of the slippers drag along the floor or the *tatami* mats. So most folks don't even realize that they are shuffling. It seems that high school boys are the worst as they walk on the backs of their shoes. So slap, slap, slap down the corridor or the sidewalk - you'd think that they have some kind of heavy shoes made of cement or something. Women wearing low heels will drag them too so you have slap, slap, slap along with the clack, clack, clack as the heel hits the ground. We *did* tell you earlier that noise is a part of Tokyo living. Such is life.

Japanese often use silence for communication as much as speaking. **DO** understand this is one method of communication. **DON'T** feel uncomfortable if there are short periods of silence when conversing with someone. **DON'T** be like the westerner who feels that every minute has to be filled with chatting.

Japanese are extremely fastidious about cleanliness. Visitors to Tokyo often remark how clean the city is and this is generally true unless one looks in some of the darker corners of the city but that is another story. This almost-fetish extends to neighbourhoods and homes. On any one morning in autumn, one will see the grandmas sweeping up the fallen leaves in front of their houses but they **DON'T** sweep even one centimetre further in front of their neighbour's house. After all one can carry this only so far! House dust and pollen, just to name two, are favourite enemies of the soap & cleaning materials companies. There are sprays, cleansers, soaps in all forms, waxes, mops, cleaning fluids blah, blah, blah. And if you believe the TV commercials, every housewife is just in *absolutely ecstasy* if her wash is whiter than white.

And personal hygiene products number in the thousands - far too numerous to mention here. Housewives will routinely wrap the lowly household garbage in small plastic bags (the kind gotten from supermarkets) and then put those in the approved garbage bag for pick up. Some even triple wrap things. However for the readers of this book, it isn't necessary to follow this obsession. **DO** just put it in the approved bag and place it at the pick-up point.

Energy drinks

Go into any drugstore and there will be one aisle completely devoted to energy drinks ranging from a hundred yen or so up to several thousand yen. Turn on any TV and one is bombarded with energy drinks commercials - guaranteed to cure what ails you - but mainly aimed at the poor sleep-deprived salaried man and that hangover

he has the morning after. However if you really want something to give you a little extra pep, try the 'elixir' made with alcohol and a curled up *mamushi* (poisonous snake) inside - of course the snake is dead but its secret juices and elixirs pass from its body into the alcohol. These drinks are supposed to make men virile and fill them with pep for you know what - although we do wonder about some of those old geezers we see drinking them. These drinks are a specialty of Okinawa by the way; that's where that poor snake comes from. So if you aren't turned off by this description **DO** go into a specialty shop and stare at all those bottles lined up on the shelves with those piecing eyes of the *mamushi* staring back out at YOU!

Neighbours

DON'T be surprised or offended if you do not become friendly with your neighbours, except for the occasional "hello, how are you" or "nice day, isn't it?" Generally Japanese do not associate with their neighbours unlike in western countries; nor do they accept non-family members into their homes except as far as the *genkan* (front door area). This is also probably one of the reasons why there are so many coffee shops or cafés. **DON'T** expect to be invited over for a beer or a cup of tea much less a barbecue. The author has lived in his neighbourhood for over 25 years and has never set foot inside any of his neighbour's houses. Having said that what do you do when someone says...

"Let's get together for dinner sometime"

In the west when someone says to another "let's get together for dinner sometime", it usually means "let's get together for dinner sometime". That sounds like an invitation doesn't it? If a Japanese person says that or "why not come over to my place sometime" what he/she really means is "I hope that we can be friendly and can get along well together." Sounds confusing? Hmmmm. In a word or two, Japanese just do not invite you to their home unless you are part of their group and then even so, it is still iffy if you would get an invitation. In Kansai, the greetings that are used for the invitation are so vague that what they are really saying is *not* an invitation but following more of the *honne - tatemae* principal. So the person being 'invited' can then politely decline the 'invitation.'

DO be aware of this and **DO** take any offers with a grain of salt or maybe a huge handful of salt. Unless specifics like a date and time are mentioned, **DON'T** hold your breath or you'll be holding it 'till you turn blue in the face. If you're really interested in following up on an invitation, leave your phone number, tell the person to call you anytime, but we recommend that you not sit by your phone waiting for it to ring.

However IF the invitation is genuine and you do have the opportunity to visit someone's home, then here are some tips for inviting and being invited:

***DON'T** wear tattered clothes or socks with holes when visiting someone. It can be very embarrassing when removing your shoes and your big toe is sticking out!*

It's polite to bring some food - gift-wrapped in more formal situations - or drinks when you visit someone. And it's considered polite to belittle the value of your gift or food when you offer it, even if it's blatantly untrue. **DO** *follow this custom. "It's just a little something for the kids" you can say or, "this is a little something for you and your husband".*

In more formal circumstances it's impolite to unwrap a gift someone brings you as soon as you receive it. In casual surroundings it's normal to ask the giver if it can be opened at that time.

When in the house, **DON'T** *wear your slippers into a tatami (straw) mat room.* **DO** *remove them and then step into the room.*

In a tatami mat room it's customary to sit on the floor (unless there is furniture). Men usually sit cross legged and women will sit on their legs. For the ladies, if sitting on your legs is impossible either due to the inability to do so or due to age, then it would be acceptable to rest against a wall or a sofa and stretch out one's legs. **DO** *use common sense in this situation.*

DON'T *wear your slippers into the genkan (the entrance to a home, where the shoes are kept) or outside.*

DON'T *wear the toilet room slippers outside the toilet room. Most homes keep toilet slippers in the toilet so* **DO** *follow this custom.*

DO *see a guest to the door or if in a business company to the elevator or reception desk when they leave.*

When someone visits you at home it's polite to turn their shoes around facing outward so they can be put on rather easily when leaving. When visiting however, **DO** wear shoes that are easy to slip on or if laced shoes, tie them loosely so that you can slip into them with the help of a shoehorn.

To bring this section to a close, one trait that is very common is honesty. Go to any lost and found centre of any train line and you can see not hundreds but thousands upon thousands of umbrellas all logged in and tagged, the umbrellas having been turned in. Money found on the streets is usually turned into the local police box. If no one turns up to claim it within a half year, then it belongs to the finder. If claimed then the finder is entitled to a finder's fee, usually 10 percent.

Stories abound of people having become well off due to found money never claimed. Back in the 70s, there was a man who, while out walking in Tokyo, found a *furoshiki* (cloth wrapping) filled with ¥100,000,000 by the side of the road. It was never claimed and after the required waiting time, he became the owner. The required tax (about 33 percent) was deducted and a check was waiting for him. Out jogging one early morning, he showed up at the police box and collected the check worth some ¥66,000,000, a nice sum of money in those days - not a bad payday in all! So despite what one reads in the papers about dishonest politicians taking their cut or tax cheats or others manipulating the stock markets, the moral of this story is that the Japanese do have a penchant for honesty.

FESTIVALS AND HOLIDAYS

Japan, like many other countries in Asia, is a land of festivals and it surprises visitors as to how pagan they can be. There are festivals that are celebrated throughout the country and then there are local festivals special to a region or city. You know that you aren't in Ohio anymore when you see thousands of half naked men dancing in the streets while beating wildly on drums. You'll see idols and shrines that house many different gods and giant phalluses being paraded through the streets in front of women and children.

Festivals are a fantastic opportunity to see this country that in some ways has largely disappeared. We recommend that if you have the time and chance you go and see some of these unusual reminders of past traditions and ceremonies. It is virtually impossible to cover them all so we'll look at the main ones and some others that are a little different. We have taken a seasonal approach as a lot of the festivals have their origins in the seasons or the calendar and the universe.

Winter (December to March)

Oshogatsu (New Year's) is a special time of year. Young people up to 19 years are given little packets of money and on New Year's Day, folks usually go to a shrine to pray for what they wish in the New Year. Families usually get together and most people in large cities return to their home towns, creating huge traffic jams upwards of 30km on major thoroughfares. Rail and air services are fully packed, with trains filled to 200 percent capacity. Conversely, the large cities, should you wish not to travel at this time, become quite pleasant, quiet and easy to get around. If driving, one can actually get through three or four green lights in one shot without stopping. **DO** stay in the city if you want some peace and quiet and no crowds!

Setsubun no Hi Festival (February)

"Devils out" - "Good luck (enter) in" (the house). This festival has its origins in old the lunar calendar that designates the end of winter on the 2nd or 3rd. Dried beans are thrown as they are believed to be a source for the impregnation of the earth and therefore are thrown to scare off any devils still lurking after winter. While some shrines still follow this festival, nowadays it's mostly children who have a lot of fun throwing the beans at imaginary devils.

White Day (March 14)

Everybody or mostly everybody celebrates Valentine's Day but Japan and only Japan has White Day. Please **DO** note. *In Japan it is the women who give chocolates to the men on Valentine's Day.* Not only will the ladies give some chocolate to their special person or lover, they will also give chocolate, known as *giri chocolate* (or obligatory chocolate) to those men they may work with in the office. So corporate Japan wanting to boost the sales of chocolate and chocolate related products, invented White Day. On White Day, it is the man's turn to give something in return. So fellows, **DO** note the difference and **DO** give your special lady some luxury chocolates. All the major and famous chocolatiers depend on these two days for a major portion of their annual sales.

Spring (April to June)

Hanami (Cherry Blossom Viewing)

Ah, spring time... the thoughts of warm weather after the long winter... cherry blossoms in full bloom splashing the city in shades of pink... women in *kimonos* along with men sitting under the beautiful cherry trees sipping Japanese sake and reading poetry. If these are your thoughts **DO** take a reality check. Go to any major park at the height of the season and you will be inundated with crowds, men and women sitting on blue plastic sheets spread on the ground, karaoke boxes and people singing and clapping along, men (and the ladies too!) sprawled out on those plastic sheets in a semi-drunken state, some guy over in the bushes taking a leak - oops watch out for the little pool of vomit - and garbage... did we

mention the garbage?...garbage, garbage everywhere and all the parks did stink. Ueno park, which has some of the most beautiful cherry trees becomes for a few nights every year one of the ugliest sites in the city.

> So what to do if you want to avoid those crowds during cherry blossom season? We recommend that you find a place in your neighbourhood, gather a few friends and have a small party. **DO** avoid the large parks and other well known sites that have cherry trees.

Golden Week Vacation

This week is comprised of three national holidays which strung together with perhaps another weekday or the weekend, make a long break. The national holidays are April 29th or Green Day (this was the former Emperor's birthday), May 3rd or Constitution Day and May 5th or Children's Day. May 4th is a regular working day but most companies let their workers take it as a personal day. It is at this time that you will see colourful paper carp kites being flown from houses or balconies that have children. The carp, a strong fish and one that can swim up river or against the current, represents the wish for strong and healthy children. So add on the weekend before (as applicable) and the one on the end, and you have a long holiday.

Like New Year's, there is a mad rush out of anywhere to somewhere! Rail, air, road, stage coaches, carts or all kinds, in fact anything on wheels is pressed into service in moving the population to wherever it is going. **DO** avoid all major airports unless absolutely necessary and **DO** stay off the expressways unless you are prepared to sit in traffic. If however it is not avoidable, **DO** prepare some adult and/or children's paper diapers just in case you get stuck in a long line of traffic and the nearest rest area is 20km down the road. Early May is a very pleasant season and with some careful planning, one can have a nice holiday by staying in the city or having a barbecue on the Tama River or just chilling out at home with a mint julep or whatever your druthers are.

Hamamatsu Matsuri (May 3rd - 5th)

Held in Shizuoka Prefecture, more than 150 teams compete in a kind of kite fighting where giant kites are flown into other kites in order to cut the strings of the other - sort of like King of the Mountain. Many of the kites are as large as three to five meters and it is said that it takes the greater part of a year to construct them. The kites are colourful and show a lot of creativity.

Aoi Festival

If you want to see some of old style Kyoto, May 15th marks the day of the Aoi festival also known as the Kamo festival. It is held at both the Kamigamo and Shimogamo Shrines. The origin of the festival dates back to the time of the Kinmei Emperor (approximately 1,400 years ago). The grain at the time was not ripening, and this was seen as a curse from the Kamo-god. A horse was made to run through the streets with bells attached, and an abundant harvest resulted. This tradition continued unbroken and came to be celebrated on a grand scale from the Fujiwara era. The name of the Aoi Festival originated from the tradition of offering geraniums (*aoi*) to the gods, and decorating the temple, attendees and ox carriages with geranium leaves. Wearing elegant costumes of the Ocho era, the refined charm of the envoy and public servants parading through the city represents old-style Kyoto.

Summer (July to September)

Umi no Hi (Marine Day)

This is a relatively new national holiday held on the third Monday of July. There are no special events but July being summer, folks flock to the beach. In Kanto area (Tokyo & its surrounding environs) the beaches south and east of Tokyo are jammed. **DO** get there early and get your patch of sand. This three day weekend is marked by the usual fireworks displays somewhere, lost kids, drunken guys and their girlfriends, surfers of all ages and styles, sunbathers, barbecue parties and more garbage...didn't we mention garbage before someplace??

Fireworks

Summer is a season of fireworks displays in July and August. They are elaborately staged and huge crowds converge on the best spots to watch. **DO** check your local newspaper for the dates and locations of these displays.

Gion Festival, Kyoto (July 1 - 31)

This festival, one of the three largest in Japan, along with the Kanda Festival in Tokyo and the Tenjin Festival in Osaka, lasts for almost a month. With the ceremonial Mikoshiarai (washing of the portable shrines) on the 10th through to the Kankou Festival on the 24th as its centrepiece, it spreads over the whole of Kyoto's Shijo-douri. This festival began approximately 1,100 years ago when, as a prayer for the end of plague, 66 pikes (one for each of the provinces) were made and sent with portable shrines to Shinsen-en. Then from modern times, textile workers and merchants using their cultural expertises created the dazzling Yamaboko floats during the Edo era. These may still be seen today. Then the *kon-chiki-chin* Gion Rhythm (*Gion-bayashi*) is played in each town where the pikes are made. The festival reaches its peak on the 17th, with the Yamaboko Float Parade (*Yamaboko Jyunkou*).

Aomori Nebuta Festival (August 2 - 7)

Another famous festival is the Aomori Nebuta Festival. A *nebuta* float, made with a wooden base and upper frames over which Japanese rice paper is shaped into figures and glued onto the frames, is pulled through the streets of Aomori. These shapes are either Japanese historical figures or Kabuki characters and are extremely colourful and a photographer's delight.

Obon Holiday

Obon usually lasts about three days during the middle of August. These days mark the occasion when Japanese return to their home towns to welcome back the departed souls of their ancestors. Fruit and drinks and other food items are set out for the returning spirits

at the start of Obon and families gather together perhaps to visit their ancestors' graves, wash the gravestone, place flowers and incense before it and pray for the departed. After that all gather for a small party at home or perhaps at a local restaurant. And *once again*, people leave the cities in droves so **DO** read what we wrote for New Year's and Golden Week vacations.

Gozan Fire Festival (August 16th, from 8:00 p.m.)

This tradition, said to have been started by the monk Kobo-Daishi when praying for an end to plague, lights up the surrounding skies of Kyoto with the character *dai* (large). Fire beds are prepared and lit halfway up the mountains that surround Kyoto. The three strokes of the character can be seen from every

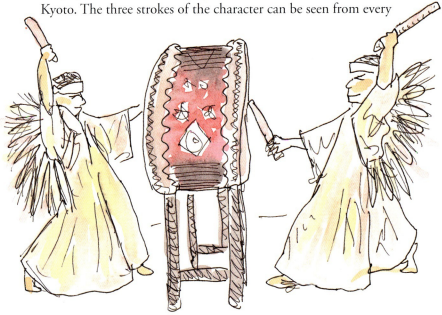

part of the city. The five fires on Gozan - Daimonji, Myoho, Funagata, Hidari-daimonji and Torii-gata - are lit simultaneously, painting the night sky a bright red and creating one of Kyoto's most memorable summer scenes while marking the end of the Obon season.

Danjiri Festival (September 14th & 15th)

This festival is said to have originated in 1703 as a harvest festival. The floats showing scenes from famous battles are intricately carved and each one is owned by a different neighbourhood. There are a total of 30 different floats and they are pulled around the neighbourhoods relatively slowly. If perchance one float meets another then things can get rather rough and they are rammed into one another. On the 15th, the floats are pulled through the streets by a team of drunken men but along the same routes. This time it is a race to see which float can go the fastest. These things can weigh up to four tons and have a very high centre of gravity, thereby making them very unstable on corners. And on top of these floats are three or four people riding them like a surf board while encouraging their team to go faster. Broken bones and other injuries are not unheard of. **DO** go see this festival and bring your camera.

Autumn (October to November)

Jidai Festival (October 22nd)

This festival was started in the 28th year of the Meiji era (1895) when the 1,100th anniversary of Heian Sento (the relocation of the capital) was celebrated. In the morning, the shrine procession travels from the Heian Shrine to the Kyoto Imperial Palace, and at noon, processions representing each era parade through the city, and return to the Heian Shrine. Over the course of one hour, the evolution of cultural items and clothing over 1,000 years is recreated. In the Edo era procession, old-styles and interesting items of clothing belonging to the Yarimochi, Kasamochi, Kyosekimochi and Warajitori clans can be seen.

And now to some different festivals sure to tickle your funny bone or whatever other bone you may have in your body...

Kanamara Matsuri Festival (April 15th)

Held every year at Wakamiya Hachimangu Shrine in Kawasaki, this festival is about as wild and pagan as they get. This festival is said to celebrate the vanquishing of a demon that lived in a woman's vagina and who would bite off the penises of her lovers! So according to legend, a local craftsman fashioned a steel phallus which broke the demon's teeth. People of all ages participate in a parade. In this parade you will see participants sporting huge penises, and a giant phallus is carried through the street. Females will ride on a phallus shaped seesaw and everybody, including men, women and children, will be sure to get their picture taken embracing a phallic statue. For souvenirs, you can buy candies shaped as penises and other such phallic paraphernalia.

In the Edo period this festival was especially important in that courtesans would come to pray for business and for protection from venereal diseases. The whole festival is presided over by a Shinto priest who carries out traditional and secret rituals and prayers. Many women nowadays take part in the festival in order to pray for conception during their marriage.

And another one...

Tagata-Jinja Hounen Matsuri (March 15th)

This particular festival is held at the Tagata-Jinja (shrine) in Komaki City, Aichi Prefecture. A large wooden phallus, measuring eight feet long and weighing up to 1,000 pounds is carried around on a *mikoshi* (portable shrine). There are other phalluses available for touching, also phallic shaped candy and goodies and small souvenirs. The shrine itself is lined with phalluses. And in this era of equal opportunity and gender equality, there is a vagina festival one week later.

Now back to nakedness...

Hadaka Matsuri (February 17th)

While *hadaka* means nakedness, the participants aren't strictly naked because they do dress in loin cloths. In this festival held at Konomiya Shrine in Inazawa, Aichi Prefecture, participants pursue a naked man trying to touch him as he passes by. This 'naked man' is a kind of scapegoat who absorbs evil and it is thought that he will bring good luck to anyone touching him. The festival itself is well over 1,200 years old and it attracts more than 10,000 runners and well over 300,000 spectators. There is usually heavy drinking resulting in injuries.

Another *hadaka matsuri* is held on January 14th in Kyoto at Hino Hokai-ji temple. In this festival, loin clothed participants sing chants and rub against one another. We are not too sure of the significance of the rubbing but it sure heats things up for the participants!

Black and blue...

Takeuchi Matsuri (February 15th)

The people of Rokugo town in Akita Prefecture divide themselves into two teams and whack each other with long bamboo poles. Why they are whacking each other, we are not entirely sure but this festival fits into the "only in Japan" category! Of course the men wear helmets (to protect themselves) but after the first two or three minutes, this festival goes into extended rounds and anything goes. The poles are thrown down and the participants then go at it with fists, elbows, knees, anything that is hard. Needless to say, hospitals and clinics do rather brisk business after this festival.

On pins and needles...

Hari Kuyo (late January or early February)

This one may seem a bit odd but in days gone by, pins and needles were among a woman's most important possessions. This is not strictly a festival but more of a memorial service for all bent pins and/or broken needles. The pins and needles are inserted into a pan of tofu while prayers are recited over them. The *tofu* is then wrapped in paper and floated down a river or put out to sea. Some temples that hold this service are: Shojuin Temple near Shinjuku Gyoen-mae station, Shinganji Temple near Shimokitazawa Station and Sensoji Temple in Asakusa, all in Tokyo.

And a few other different events...

Naki-zumo or "Ko-naki-zumo" ("Crying Sumo")

Crying *sumo*?? What's that you say? Huge *sumo* wrestlers actually crying? Is this some kind of new sport?

Well not exactly. Differing in time of year and actual procedures, Naki-zumo is held in various places including Momiyama in Tochigi and Hirado in Nagasaki where babies are jostled or thrown up in the air to see which one will cry first and loudest and longest. The adults doing the throwing are men wearing only *sumo mawashi* or belts and the babies are dressed in little

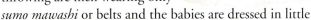

half coats and wear a headband. The baby who is 'first' in crying wins the contest and it is believed that this will bring good health to the crier or a good harvest to the village where it is held. And in some places, actual *sumo* rings (*dohyo*) are used in this contest.

Wanko-soba eating contest

This is not exactly a festival but is equivalent to a hot dog eating contest in the USA. It's a special of Iwate and is held at various times throughout the year. This contest is every *soba*-lover's fantasy. Waitresses stand behind each sitting contestant, holding a tray full of small bowls and each containing a mouthful of soba. They then keep dumping the *soba* bowls into the contestant's eating bowl. These waitresses are well trained so that as soon as the contestant finishes one helping, before he can blink he'll find another one dumped in his bowl. The only way one can stop this cycle is by putting a lid on the bowl, but this has to be done after one has emptied it - for courtesy demands that one eats what is served - thus making it into a hectic chase,

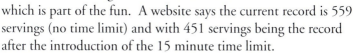

which is part of the fun. A website says the current record is 559 servings (no time limit) and with 451 servings being the record after the introduction of the 15 minute time limit.

Namahage Festival (February 13-15)

"Are there any cry babies in this house?" shout the Ogres. On December 31 in the town of Oga in Akita Prefecture, men wearing fearsome red or blue demon-like masks, dressed up in straw coats and carrying big knives and wooden buckets, come down from Mr. Shinzan into the town. They then go from house to house looking for lazy children and even adults and threatening them with their knives. Needless to say they are quite successful at scaring the living daylights out of the children who usually end up crying and cowering in fear at these ogres. It is all meant in good fun however, but try telling the kids that. This festival is re-enacted for the general public in the grounds of Shinzan Shrine in February.

The Japan International Birdman Rally

Usually held the last weekend in July, this rally is one of the most unusual, and we should say exciting contests held in Japan. The contestants are usually university students and engineers employed by regular companies. They compete to see who can build and fly the best HPV or human powered vehicle across Lake Biwa. These vehicles are made of super lightweight materials and usually have wingspans exceeding 30 meters or so. Launched from a ten meter high platform, some of them fly like eagles while others plunge dramatically into the lake. The operator must control the pitch and direction of the craft, all very delicate operations, while pedalling as fast as he can! The 2005 winner was the Nihon University Aero Student Group and their craft flew 22,813.05 meters. This distance unfortunately was not a new record due to unusually strong winds that day.

In addition to the HPV there are two other categories, Gliders and the 'challenge category' where the look and design of the craft are more important than the actual distance flown. This rally is held on Matsubara beach on the shores of Lake Biwa. Lake Biwa is located about an hour by train from Kyoto.

RELIGION

Japan

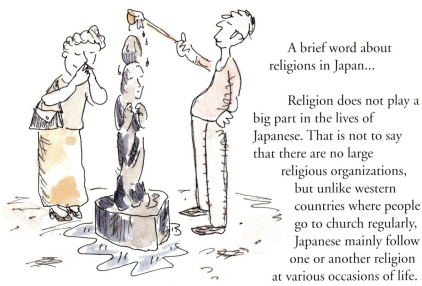

A brief word about religions in Japan...

Religion does not play a big part in the lives of Japanese. That is not to say that there are no large religious organizations, but unlike western countries where people go to church regularly, Japanese mainly follow one or another religion at various occasions of life. Generally speaking, Shintoism and its ceremonies are called upon for congratulatory events of life and Buddhism for the more serious events, such as death and remembrance of departed ones in memorial ceremonies.

Is that a temple or a shrine in front of you? If there is a *torii* or Japanese gate, then it is a Shinto shrine, the gate being symbolic of the separation between this life and the *kami* or gods. In Shintoism two deities named Izanagi-no-mikoto and Izanami-no-mikoto gave birth to the Japanese islands. Between them they had a daughter named Amaterasu Omikami (Sun Goddess) who is believed to be the ancestress of the Imperial Family and is the chief deity. Her shrine is located in Ise. Shinto accepts the basic tenet that there are *kami* (gods) in all

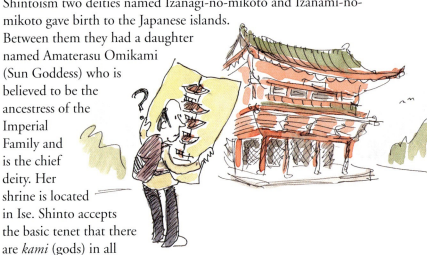

things and recognizes that there are sacred places such as mountains and springs that are special to these gods. Animals are messengers of the *kami* and upon entering a shrine you will see two guard dogs facing each other.

At births, graduations, marriages, building a house, an opening ceremony of any kind and other congratulatory events of life, **DO** accept the services of a Shinto priest so the proper ceremony will be carried out.

On the other hand, Buddhism came from Korea in 522 and has developed over the centuries, having been shaped by Japanese cultural practices and values. It has developed differently from the Buddhism practiced elsewhere in Asia. In temples you will find images of the Buddha and all of the different and divine beings that are associated with Buddhism.

For funerals and services for the departed, a Buddhist priest will perform a memorial service as requested. This usually involves the chanting of *sutras* to the beating of a drum and the ringing of chimes. Incense is offered for the departed by all those participating. **DO** read our section on funerals for more detail. During *Obon* season - usually mid-August - Japanese will return to their hometowns to welcome back the departed spirits of their ancestors. While this is a time for family gatherings, it is also a time for services for the departed so Buddhist traditions are followed at this time. If invited to such a ceremony, formal wear or dress - usually black - is required and a small gift of money is presented as well. After the gathering, all will go to a nearby restaurant or perhaps return home for an appropriate meal with drinks.

A well known aspect of Buddhism is Zen Buddhism. Zen was first introduced to the western world by the author D.T. Suzuki. Suffice it to say that there are many Zen temples throughout Japan. These temples are the outward mirror of Zen principles and of Zen mind. A visit to one is truly an uplifting experience. Zen cannot be transmitted in books. Phrases like, "no mind" and "everything is Zen" and then again, "nothing is Zen" all add to the confusion. To put it simply, Zen means meditation and meditation cannot be transmitted in books. Meditation is practice - the simple and at the same time the most difficult practice of applying one's backside to a cushion, crossing one's legs and emptying one's mind of all attachments - to achieve 'no mind.'

There are many stories or jokes however that poke fun at Buddhist monks because they 'charge' for all these services and the more famous the monk the higher the charge. There are stories of monks who ride around in Mercedes Benz's as they make their rounds to various funerals or memorial services. A parody of funerals and the monks who make money from them was done by Juzo Itami in his movie, *Osooshiki* (Funeral). In it, the monk arrives for the required ceremony in a Rolls Royce driven by a chauffeur and is dressed in very gaudy, rich looking robes. All the members of the household are very deferential and show him the utmost respect.

But the reader should be aware that there are indeed many monks who live simple lives taking care of their temples and the people who support that temple. So **DO** take these stories with a grain of salt.

Christianity is not really part of the social fabric. Christianity was brought to Japan in the 16th century but its followers were severely restricted and openly persecuted. Nowadays there are both Catholic and Protestant churches run by Japanese and foreign pastors sprinkled throughout the major cities. When looking for a church of your following, **DO** look in the English telephone books that are published by NTT (the phone company).

New Year is a special time for most people and there is the custom of *hatsumode* when lots of people dress up in kimonos and visit either temples or shrines to offer a coin and say a prayer for the New Year. It is a festive occasion and at the larger temples and shrines there are stalls selling toys, different types of finger foods, children's masks and games. However the original purpose of these visits is to offer prayers for what you wish in the New Year. So if you are in Japan at this time of year, **DO** join the crowds and follow this traditional custom.

Yamabushi are very strict religious ascetics who literally live in the mountains. This sect, known as the *Shingon* sect, is an offshoot of esoteric Buddhism. The men become hermits and study nature, spiritual texts and martial arts and they are known for their spiritual and mystical abilities. Needless to say this style of life is not for everybody.

Japan is no stranger to cults either, witness the *Aum Shinrikyo* and its attempt to poison the public with its sarin gas attacks in the Tokyo subway system in 1995. This cult has effectively been abandoned and now operates under a new name and 'reformed' policy although its movements are watched by the police. Its original founder is incarcerated. There have been other cults as well that have basically stolen from their followers by charging high prices for services or for jewellery or amulets and other so-called 'power' objects. These groups have only served the interests of their founders and usually have been exposed for what they really represent.

And on to Weddings and Funerals.....

It is really quite easy to get married in Japan. Simply go to the city or ward office, fill out the required documents and the union is complete - as simple as that. No ceremony, no honeymoon, no nothing! However nowadays most couples do opt for a ceremony of some kind and this may include the traditional Shinto ceremony with only the relatives of each side present, or a western style ceremony done by a minister or pastor or a westerner *acting* as a minister and held in a wedding chapel that may be located nearby.

Nowadays there are companies that can arrange

all of the ceremonies and they have 'ministers' on call, usually westerners, wearing the proper robes, who will perform the 'ceremony.' Some westerners make a business out of this profession and while the westerner is a fake minister, the couple wants all the trappings of the ceremony and so sign up for a package deal. You may say, "well, isn't this a sham?" Yes, true - but from the Japanese point of view, the couple is creating a memory of their union and so it is part of the show on this very special day. It is not looked down upon in any way whatsoever. After the ceremonies comes the reception.

Weddings are an enterprise unto themselves and competition is fierce. Riding any public transport one will see poster advertisements for wedding halls, wedding packages and honeymoons. Banquets are held in wedding halls, hotels, or restaurants and the more guests invited the greater the status. Sometimes there are very few guests and so to fill out the tables, people known as *benriya* may be hired for the day to act as a friend or classmate or long lost acquaintance of the bride or the groom. These people will study the background of that person's family and schooling so that they can carry on a conversation with others at the banquet. Of course they are paid for their services.

DO arrive prior to the time noted on the invitation. There is always a reception desk for the invited guests where you will write your name and address and leave an envelope of money. Cash is the accepted gift but it is quite a debate in Japanese society as to how much is enough. The cash is inserted into envelopes bought at any convenience store. These envelopes are very decorative in red and white, congratulatory colours. Your money will help defray the cost of the celebrations unless of course dad has agreed to foot the whole bill and in that case, the cash will be used to set up the new household.

If one has a lot of relatives with children, going to weddings can be quite an expensive undertaking over a long period of time as those children grow and get married! So we hope you have deep pockets.

DO dress in formal wear - men in suits, either morning suits or business suits, and white ties; and women in their best clothes or *kimonos*.

Seating is always predetermined with the groom's relatives and friends on one side of the room and the bride's on the other side.

Banquets are choreographed quite carefully by the couple with the caterer. There will be an MC who will move things along and introduce speakers and the various stages of the banquet.

The bride may go through a couple of changes of clothes during the banquet. She will leave and then re-enter at the appropriate time with lights doused and music blaring. The more changes of clothes, the more expensive the wedding.

DO offer toasts to all and **DO** bring a camera for lots and lots of pictures.

DO say *omedetou gozaimasu* (congratulations) as the couple nears your table.

There will be speeches on both sides, usually someone close to the couple. In the case of the groom, the speaker may be his boss or a former classmate. These speeches are usually a bit on the far side of reality and are meant to add to the festivity of the occasion. Exaggeration is not spared at all!

The banquet will usually involve several courses with drinks so **DO** pace yourself during the entire affair.

Banquets start and finish on time as noted on the invitation so **DO** leave when the event is finished.

A small gift will be presented to each person upon exiting as a token of thanks for attending. The couple along with their relatives will line up by the door and express their thanks with bows for your attendance. **DO** graciously accept the gift and offer congratulations as you approach them.

When the formal banquet is finished, the couple may then have a *nijikai* or second and informal get together with friends at a local lounge. If invited, **DO** feel free to attend as this is a lot of fun with drinks flowing along with good conversation and laughs. Usually the immediate relatives do not attend this second get-together.

Funerals

While not the happiest of topics, there are several dos & don'ts concerned with death. The services of Buddhist priests are requested for funerals and memorial services. In days past, funerals were held in the homes of the deceased but due to urban living or privacy issues, families will have the funeral at a local temple (if available) or at one of the public funeral halls found in the city. The entire mourning period is comprised of two parts, that of the wake and the funeral. The wake is usually attended by family, friends, colleagues etc. of the deceased whereas usually, but not exclusively, only family members and close friends will attend the funeral.

Wedding tie

Funeral tie

In Japan cremation is the rule. It takes place after the funeral service and all members go to the crematorium and wait in a sitting room while the deceased is being cremated. Snacks, soft drinks, beer and Japanese sake are served to those waiting. If the family owns a burial plot, the ashes will be interred at a later date. In case there is no family plot, the family will have a small altar at home with the ashes kept in an urn in the center of the altar.

If required to attend a funeral, **DO** observe the following:

DO wear black formal wear or when this is not possible, a suit or appropriate clothing with a black armband or black tie.

DO prepare a gift of money called *okoden*. This gift is placed in a black bordered envelope - also available at any convenience store - and is presented at the reception desk where you will write your name and address. If you're unsure how much to give, **DO** ask an acquaintance or colleague.

The ceremony will commence with the entrance of the

Buddhist priest who will sit at the front before the closed casket and begin to chant sutras. There will be the beating of a drum and the ringing of a chime. This will continue for about 30 or 40 minutes. During this time, all mourners will line up - there will be ushers guiding everybody - in order to offer incense before the deceased's casket. Upon approaching the front, bow to the immediate family members who will be seated on the right and to the more distant family members seated on the left and then bow to the deceased's photo that is placed above the casket. After that grasp a little incense with your forefingers, raise it to your forehead (but do not touch your forehead) and then place it on the coals. **DO** this three times. Then *gassho* or place your hands together and offer a prayer for the deceased. This will last for a minute or so. When finished, turn and bow once again to the deceased and then to the relatives on the right and on the left and return to your seat. **DO** follow the usher's guidance.

Upon completion of the ceremony and upon exiting, you will be given a small gift as a token of thanks for your attendance. One of the things in the bag will be a small packet of salt. Before you enter the front door of your own home, sprinkle or throw the salt over your shoulders as it is meant to cleanse you from the 'bad vibes' or bad luck of the funeral.

When the prayer ceremony is finished, the mourners will gather in a separate room for a very light meal and something to drink, either soft or alcoholic. **DO** partake of this repast and at an appropriate time, **DO** take your leave. Nothing further is necessary.

And after an appropriate time, you will receive a small gift from perhaps a department store as a remembrance of your visit to the funeral. It is not necessary to make a return gift.

When one dies in Japan, a family member's obligation continues for a rather long time since memorial services are held at intervals of one year, two years, six years and then twelve years. These memorial services are usually only for family members and close friends of the deceased.

DOING BUSINESS

They say that doing business in Japan can be equivalent to getting through a minefield but it really isn't all that difficult if some common sense is used and one learns some etiquette and procedures. Assuming that this may be your first visit to Japan, **DO** prepare thoroughly for your meeting with your business partners. If you can send information in advance **DO** so. This should include details concerning the matter to be discussed, the more detailed the better including your company profile. **DO** prepare everything on company paper or letterhead for the best impression. Bring sufficient copies with you for all members who may be present. More than likely you will have someone with whom you will be corresponding. So details such as who will be present, titles or positions and number of those attending can all be discovered in advance. Then sufficient preparations can be made on your side. Easy!

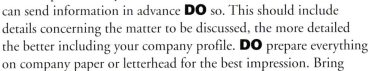

Business dress is normal business wear, as seen in any big city. Casual wear should be avoided unless the setting is other than a conference or meeting room.

Business cards are a must but it is not necessary to have them done in both languages. When first meeting your counterpart, **DO** present your card with both hands extended and receive your counterpart's in the same manner. Look at the card; **DON'T** immediately put it away in your pocket or some other place. **DON'T** be like the crass American who went to a business meeting after lunch and then during the meeting, used his counterpart's business card to clean his teeth and then folded it and put it in his pocket. Needless to say, he never got the order.

Most Japanese will shake hands with foreigners so **DO** not expect that you have to bow. But if meeting a senior official who does bow, **DO** return the bow with both hands at your sides and at the same angle as the official's bow. **DON'T** glad hand or back slap or use anybody's first name. **DO** treat your counterpart with respect. This holds true for both male and female visitors.

The Business Meeting

As you are led into the meeting room **DO** stand and wait until all are assembled and then present your business card to the most senior person who will normally sit at the head of the table. If you are the ranking senior person as well, you will be seated across from him. Introductions will be made all around and cards exchanged accordingly. Then all will sit down. What to do with all these business cards? Carefully arrange them in front of you, in the same order as the Japanese side is sitting. This not only helps to put a face to a name but is also a reminder of the hierarchy.

If the meeting is held in a smaller room with only a few participants, you as the visitor will sit on the couch and the Japanese side will sit in the individual chairs. *All* rooms are laid out in this fashion with a low table in the centre.

If there is no one on the Japanese side who is conversant in your language, then more than likely an interpreter will be arranged. If an interpreter is arranged for, then **DO** address all your remarks to the interpreter for translation while at the same time talking as directly as possible to the most senior person.

DO make frequent eye contact with the senior person but **DON'T** assume that the translator will be a decision maker just because he speaks your language; and **DON'T** try to 'buddy up' to the translator thinking that

he may have some inside track. All final decisions will be deferred to the most senior person. If required to make a presentation, break up your presentation into short segments allowing for the possibility that re-explanation may be necessary. When answering questions, **DO** keep your answers directed to the matter at hand and **DON'T** wander in your reply as this may cause misinterpretation or miscommunication. Humour is best avoided at the first stage as it may not be appreciated due to cultural differences.

If this is the first meeting, then there will be interest from the Japanese about you as a person, your country, where you live and so on but there won't be anything personal. You may be asked your age at some stage so **DON'T** take offence at this. This is a very normal thing in Japan. Show mutual interest in the same topics as you are asked and **DO** show your human side as well.

DO be thoroughly prepared. This cannot be stressed enough. The Japanese will do the same so if you need to bring an expert on your new widget then **DO** so that he/she can thoroughly answer all questions with knowledge and confidence. **DON'T** think you can wing it as this will leave a very bad impression. **DO** go to the extra expense of bringing another person.

DON'T get impatient or even *show* impatience during the meeting. **DO** expect detailed discussions along with questions and an exchange of opinions. If your product is not quite suitable for the market and the Japanese side makes some suggestions, **DO** take those suggestions to heart, explaining that you will research it upon returning home to headquarters and will reply within a certain date. If changes are requested, **DO** show seriousness of purpose in explaining that you will try to make those changes. Further, **DO** explain the reasons thoroughly if changes cannot be made while at the same time offering alternative solutions.

Some light beverage, most likely tea, will be served during the meeting. In the case of a day-long meeting, lunch will be arranged so just follow the lead of your hosts. Be prepared for smoking not to be permitted in meeting rooms but if there are ashtrays present, you can assume that it is permissible to smoke but **DO** ask just in case. More than likely you will not be refused.

Negotiations may be drawn out so **DON'T** expect a decision to be made immediately. There are many cases where decisions have not come down until many weeks later. Of course if the business relationship is a long standing one, that will determine the speed of any decision. **DO** keep in mind the proverb 'patience is a virtue.' This is of utmost importance.

DO try to learn even a few words of Japanese and **DO** show some cultural understanding. While your remarks are being translated, Japanese will exclaim *"hai, hai"* many times. This means yes and it also is used as an interjection meaning, *"I am listening to you"* but it does not necessarily signal or mean agreement. So **DON'T** be like the westerner who kept hearing *"hai, hai,"* returned home and proudly told his boss that the contract was on the way. "They agreed with everything I said," he boasted. Six months later the company is still waiting for the contract.

Gifts

It is recommended to bring a gift for the most senior person and if an important client or partner, this can be something unique from your home town or something that might be a product of the area where you live, e.g., a bottle of good quality wine. **DON'T** bring something that is obviously cheap like the Texan who brought beef jerky for the CEO and exclaimed that it came from the finest cows. On the other hand **DON'T** go overboard either. **DO** think of something that will be in good taste and would be gratefully accepted. Avoid bulky gifts like those ridiculously huge desk clocks with company logos screaming from their dials: remember Japan is a small crowded country where space is very valuable. Buy something that looks (and is) quite expensive, that's either food or doesn't take up too much space, like a box of Godiva chocolates, a Parker fountain pen, or some handmade traditional craft. Remember that the Japanese have been spoiled with decades of non-stop economic growth and their tastes are rather sophisticated - they can tell whether something was bought at Macy's or at K-Mart. **DON'T** be like another American who brought magnet knick knacks for the refrigerator door. You can guess where they ended up!

On subsequent visits as you find out more about your colleagues, you can tailor your gifts to those individuals. So for example, if you learn that the boss plays golf, you could bring a box of top class golf balls next time. **DO** ensure that the gift is properly presented in nice wrapping paper. And on subsequent visits, bring something for the staff who you work with, such as sweets or the like. They will always be appreciated. **DO** present your gift(s) as the meeting draws to a close and **DO** expect that it will be returned in kind.

> *The number four is considered unlucky in Japan - the pronunciation for four and death are the same - so* **DO** *avoid any type of gift in fours such as four golf balls in one box.*

After hours

Despite the fact that you have jet lag after that 12 hour flight from Detroit or London and your eyes are bloodshot and you feel dehydrated, it is very likely that you will be invited out to dinner at the end of the day. In such cases your counterpart (along with translator) and the others at the meeting may attend. These are excellent chances to bond with your colleagues so **DO** graciously accept and **DON'T** try to beg off. The Japanese view these informal occasions as a chance to get to know you personally. And if you haven't been asked how old you are by this time, then **DO** expect the question to come up. This of course gives you the right to ask everybody else, even the ladies!

DO sample everything and show an interest in what you're eating. Prior to the start, there will be a *kanpai* or a welcome toast with a few introductory remarks. Your glass will be filled but wait until everyone's is filled and follow your host in the toast. Upon *kanpai* (equivalent to cheers when toasting), everybody will drink together. You are not expected to drink up however. If your glass is empty, someone will offer to fill it so **DO** wait for that; it is considered impolite to pour one's own drink. And likewise, you can offer to fill another's glass. **DON'T** think that you have to

empty your glass each time (that is unless you want.) If you have reached your fill and don't wish to drink any more then simply leave your glass full or take only a sip. Please be aware that you may be encouraged to get into a drinking contest but it's your call. And after this there is karaoke waiting. So what if you sound like a frog or have just came out of foggy bottom, there will always be a few English songs on the karaoke menu and 99.99999999% My Way will be one of them. Go for it and sing that song and take a bow.

> *The question sometimes comes up what one should do if you are a female visitor and you are being invited out after hours. If in a group, then there would be no reason to feel uncomfortable but if it turns out that only the inviter is doing the inviting and you might feel uncomfortable in such a situation, ask that the translator or perhaps one of the other staff be invited too. This should help to relieve any hesitations that you may have.*

Finally, you, as the guest, are not expected to pay for these dinners or outings. But if you should have a follow up meeting later on, then it is good form to invite others to your hotel for lunch or dinner on your tab of course. **DON'T** think lunch at the 'Golden Arches' - as an adventure in American culture - will

suffice though. If you do that, next time your counterparts may repay you in kind with a trip to Mosburger. You figure out what the "Mos" is...

This section cannot possibly cover all situations that you will meet so **DO** search out and read a couple of the many titles that are published on doing business in Japan.

> *What to do if you don't drink (alcohol)? If you do not drink for personal reasons such as religious beliefs or social reasons or for even reasons of health, then politely explain the reasons. You may be asked why again or the subject may come up again in a different context, so just re-explain the reasons. Your preferences will be accepted. So if you do not drink alcohol,* **DO** *order something like cold tea or a soft drink or the like. These items of course will be available at the restaurant.*

CLIMATE

Japan

Keeping in mind that there will be variations due to geographic location (from Hokkaido in the north to Okinawa in the south), the general seasons are:

Spring: late March to May

This is one of the most pleasant seasons in Japan - cherry blossom time and warm winds embrace the country.

Rainy season: June to mid-July

Rainy season is generally uncomfortable and downright miserable sometimes due to heat and high humidity. One comes to appreciate the word "muggy" during the rainy season. Umbrellas are essential so **DO** buy one and if you don't like to carry a big one purchase a folding one that will fit in a briefcase or a large handbag.

Summer: mid-July to late August

Tokyo is hot, hot, hot and due to global warming, the temperatures seem to be gradually increasing. Tokyo is also experiencing heat islands caused by tall buildings blocking offshore bay breezes from flowing into the city plus the exhaust of ubiquitous air conditioning. An A/C is a must-have unless you want to feel like a fried chicken.

Typhoon season: September to early October

Typhoons are spawned in the deep South Pacific and at the start of the season move in a general west to northwest path. Then as the season progresses they start to gradually turn north to northeast. Depending on pressure systems, they could go due west to Okinawa, Taiwan, Hong Kong or China. Kagoshima in the south of Japan seems to be right in typhoon alley as it either gets the effects of passing typhoons or gets hit directly. Needless to say it is necessary to watch the weather reports and take necessary precautions. Tokyo gets about four typhoons a year that come close enough to the city resulting in flooding of low areas, trains ceasing operations, some roofs torn off and some power outages. Typhoons are covered extensively by all TV networks.

Precautions for an approaching typhoon.

DO *keep tuned to the TV.*

While power outages are rare **DO** *have a flashlight with batteries handy.*

DO *stow away anything outside that might 'fly about' or be carried away by the strong winds such as flower pots, tools and bicycles.*

> **DO** bring in your laundry - you wouldn't want your unmentionables flying all over the neighbourhood!
>
> **DON'T** venture out - common sense but you would be surprised...
> And if your house/apartment has shutters, **DO** close them.

Autumn: October to mid-November

Considered by many to be the supreme season of all not only for the clear blue skies but also for so many autumn foods and dishes that are the signature of the season.

Winter: November to March

Tokyo doesn't really get that much snow and it seems to be getting less and less with each passing year. If it does snow, it is usually melted by midday so **DO** wait for it to clear before venturing out.

USEFUL INFO

Japan

Some Useful Information

*English available at all numbers noted below
*"0120" prefixes are toll free

Police - 110

Fire and Ambulance - 119

International calls access - 0033 or 010

International operator assisted calls - 0051

Operator Assistance (NTT, East domestic) - 0120-019116

St. Luke's International Hospital - (03) 3541-5151

Tokyo Adventist Hospital - (03) 3392-6151

AIDS Hotline - 0120-461995

Tokyo English Lifeline (TELL-multilingual anonymous counseling/information) - (03) 5774-0992

Tokyo Immigration Bureau - (03) 5796-7112

NTT publishes an English Telephone Directory, entitled Townpage available directly from NTT.

Web sites

Association of Foreign Wives in Japan (AFWJ): http://afwj.org/

Foreign Women in Japan:
　http://www.being-a-broad.com/living/living.html

Foreign Executive Women (FEW): http://www.fewjapan.com/

College Women's Association of Japan (CWAJ):

　http://www.cwaj.org/

Gaijin Pot (Forum for foreigners): http://www.gaijinpot.com/

Metropolis Magazine: http://metropolis.japantoday.com

ELT News (Forum for English teachers):
　http://www.eltnews.com/home.shtml

Ohayo Sensei (Forum for English teachers): http://www.ohayosensei.com/

FAQ about Japan (Japan Web Guide): http://thejapanfaq.cjb.net/

Dave's ESL Cafe: http://www.eslcafe.com/

WORDS & PHRASES

Greetings

Ohayo gozaimasu	Good morning
Konnichiwa	Hello; Good afternoon
Konbanwa	Good evening
Oyaumi nasai	Good night (before sleeping)
Sayonara	Goodbye
Omedetou gozaimasu	Congratulations - New Year's greeting; birthdays; congratulatory events, etc.

General

And beginning with the most important......

Toire wa doko desuka? (toire said **toy-re**)	Where's the toilet?
Arigatou	Thanks
Domo arigatou	Thank you very much
Domoarigatou gozaimashita	Thank you very much (polite form)
Do itashimatshite	You're welcome
Osewa ni narimashita	I'm very much obliged to you
Mah-mah	So-so
Ii desu	OK, good
Dame	Not good; Stop it!
Gommenasai	I'm sorry
Moshiwake gozaimasen	I'm extremely sorry (polite form)
Sumimasen	Excuse me; I'm sorry to trouble you...
Kin'en	No smoking

Kitsuen	Smoking
Ofuro ni hairimasu	I'm going to take a bath
Sha-wa o abimasu	I'm going to take a shower
Baka	Stupid
Kawaii	Cute
Kirei	Pretty
Utsukushii	Beautiful
Sore	That
Kore	This

People and Forms of Address

Ninhonjin	Japanese
Gaikokujin	Foreigner
Amerikajin	American
Igirisujin	British
etc. etc.	
San	A suffix attached to a surname, e.g., Tanaka-san
Sama	A very polite form of 'san'
Okaasan	Mother, mom, mommy
Otoosan	Father, dad
Kodomo (tachi)	Child/children
Otokonoko	Little boy
Onnanoko	Little girl
Obasan	Aunt, auntie
Obaasan	Grandma
Ojisan	Uncle
Ojiisan	Grandpa
Tomodachi	Friend

Transportation

Densha	Train
Chikatetsu	Subway
Bah-su	Bus
Taku-shi	Taxi
Shinkansen	Bullet train
Yamanotesen	Yamanote line ('sen' = line)
Kuruma (jidoosha)	Car

Directions (to taxi driver)

Koko ni tomete kudasai	Please stop here
Migi ni magatte kudasai	Turn right please
Hidari ni magatte kudasai	Turn left please
Asoko ni orimasu	I will get off over there.

Eating/Drinking

Taberu	To eat
Tabemashoo	Let's eat or let's go eat
Nomu	To drink
Resutoran	Restaurant
Izakaya	Drinking place
Sushiya	Sushi shop
Ohashi	Chopsticks
Karai	Spicy or salty
Oishii	Good or tasty
Okanjo kudasai	Give me the bill please.

Shopping

De-pah-to	Department store
Kaimono	Shopping
Kaimono ni ikimashoo	Let's go shopping
Sore/kore wa takai desu	That's/this is expensive
Sore/kore wa yasui desu	That's/this is cheap
Ookii desu	It's big
Chiisai desu	It's small
Itadakimasu	I'll take this/that

Weather

Tenki	Weather
Atsui desu	It's hot
Samui desu	It's cold
Tenki ga ii desu	The weather's nice
Ame ga futte imasu	It's raining
Yuki ga futte imasu	It's snowing

Health

Kaze o hikimashita	I've caught a cold
Byoki desu	I'm sick/I don't feel well
Nodo ga itai	I have a sore throat
Seki ga deru	I have a cough
Itai desu	It hurts
Atama ga itai	I have a headache
Ha ga itai	I have a toothache
Onaka ga itai	My stomach hurts or is upset

Netsu ga arimasu	I have a fever
Memai suru	I feel dizzy
Oisha-san ni ikitai	I'd like to go to the doctor
Haisha-san ni ikitai	I'd like to go to the dentist
Kyukyusha o yonde kudasai	Please call an ambulance
Byooin	Hospital

Recreation

Pachinko	Pachinko
Keiba	Horse races
Yakyuu	Baseball
Ten-ni-su	Tennis
Hai-kin-gu	Hiking
Suiei	Swimming
Sok-kah	Soccer